OXFORD REVISION GUIDES

## GCSE

# PHYSICAL EDUCATION
*through diagrams*

*RoseMarie Gallagher*
*Sally Fountain*
*Linda Gee*

**OXFORD**
UNIVERSITY PRESS

# OXFORD

UNIVERSITY PRESS

Great Clarendon Street, Oxford OX2 6DP

Oxford University Press is a department of the University of Oxford.
It furthers the University's objective of excellence in research, scholarship,
and education by publishing worldwide in

Oxford   New York

Auckland   Cape Town   Dar es Salaam   Hong Kong   Karachi
Kuala Lumpur   Madrid   Melbourne   Mexico City   Nairobi
New Delhi   Shanghai   Taipei   Toronto

With offices in

Argentina   Austria   Brazil   Chile   Czech Republic   France   Greece
Gautemala   Hungary   Italy   Japan   Poland   Portugal   Singapore
South Korea   Switzerland   Thailand   Turkey   Ukraine   Vietnam

Oxford is a registered trade mark of Oxford University Press
in the UK and in certain other countries

ISBN 0 19 913399 9  School Edition
First published 1997
ISBN 0 19 913400 6  Bookshop Edition
First published 1998
15   14   13

Typesetting, artwork, and design by
Ian Foulis & Associates, Plymouth, Devon.
Additional artwork by Ian Heard.

Front cover photograph by John P Kelly/Image Bank.

The authors would like to thank Jem Nicholls for his constructive
criticism and advice.

Printed in Great Britain.

# Contents

# Preparing for revision

Successful revision starts here, with a little preparation ...

**GO**

*... tomorrow ...
I think I'll begin
tomorrow ...*

### 1 What do I need to revise?
- If you don't know, get a copy of the PE exam syllabus.
- You can ask your teacher for one, or contact your exam board.

### 2 How is the exam structured?
- That depends on the exam board you are enrolled with.
- There is a practical test and a written paper. There may also be a project.
- The written paper usually accounts for 30 or 40% of the marks.
- Find the answers to these questions by asking your teacher or looking in the syllabus:

> *How many components are there altogether, in the PE exam?*
>
> *How many marks for each?*
>
> *What will I be tested on, in the practical test?*
>
> *How long is the written paper?*

### 3 How shall I plan my revision?
- Start revising at least three months before the exam. (But better late than never ...)
- A revision timetable will help you make the most of your time.
- Make a large timetable like the one started below, and fill it in for all your subjects.

### The PE exam syllabus
- It will tell you all about the PE exam, and what you need to know for it.
- The syllabus may look quite complex. If you don't understand it, ask someone to explain it to you.

### Contacting your exam board
**London:** University of London Examinations and Assessment Council, Stewart House, 32 Russell Square, London WC1B 5DN.
Tel 0171 331 4000

**MEG:** Midland Examining Group, Syndicate Buildings, 1 Hills Road, Cambridge CB1 2EU.
Tel 01223 553 311

**NEAB:** Northern Examinations and Assessment Board, 12 Harter Street, Manchester M1 6HL.
Tel 0161 953 1180

**SEG:** Southern Examining Group, Stag Hill House, Guildford, Surrey GU2 5XJ.
Tel 01483 506 506

**SQA:** Scottish Qualifications Authority, Ironmills Road, Dalkeith, Midlothian EH22 1LE.
Tel 0131 663 6601

**WJEC:** Welsh Joint Education Committee, 245 Western Avenue, Cardiff CF5 2YX.
Tel 01222 561 231

**CCEA:** Northern Ireland Council for the Curriculum Examinations and Assessment, Clarendon Dock, 29 Clarendon Road, Belfast BT1 3BG
Tel 01232 261 200

## REVISION TIMETABLE

| Week starting: | Weeks to exam: | MON | TUE | WED | THU |
|---|---|---|---|---|---|
| 7 March | 12 | PE 4 – 5.30<br>FRENCH 6.30 – 8.00 | | | |
| 14 March | 11 | | | | |

# Revision time!

The secret of revision is: **work smart!**
This page shows how you to be smart about revision.

## You'll need ...
- this book
- the PE syllabus
- your class notes, or PE textbook, for further reading
- plenty of paper to write on
- a pen or pencil, or several in different colours, and a highlighting pen if you have one.

## Using this book
- Each page in this book is a revision unit.
- You do not need to work through every unit. It depends on your syllabus.
- So first, check the contents list against the syllabus and tick the units you must cover.
- Then work through these units. Tick them again as you complete them.

## The question bank
- Answering questions helps you revise.
- The question bank contains one exam-level question, or sometimes two, for each revision unit.
- Look for the signpost at the foot of the unit. It will direct you to the right question.

  For example:   Q3, page 79

- Answers are given at the back of the book.

## How to revise a topic
Reading is not enough. Revision means **action!** So ...
- Make **notes**. Write down the main headings for the topic, and list key points below them. Use a different colour for the headings. Highlighting makes points easier to remember.
- Make **spider maps**. These are a good way to revise.
- **Test yourself**. Check you know a diagram by covering up the labels. Answer questions from the question bank, and check your answers in the Answer section.
- **Repeat**. Look at your revision notes again, at intervals. For example at the end of the revision session, next day, a week later and so on. This will help you remember everything.
- **Ask for help**. If you don't understand something, don't waste too long on it. Ask your teacher for help.

## Be nice to your brain!
- Your brain gets less effective at absorbing information after about 40 minutes.
- So take frequent short breaks. Stretch, walk about, leap around, dance.

## The revision spot
- Choose a quiet place where you can concentrate. Not in front of the TV!
- It should be well lit, to help your eyes.

## Making spider maps
- Turn a sheet of paper sideways.
- Write the name of the topic in a circle in the middle of the page, as shown below.
- Then write in the main headings with spider links to the circle.
- If you can't think of headings, *What, Why, Where, How, When* are a good start!
- Write in the key points and make links as shown.
- Use different colours for different parts of the map.
- The result is a summary of the topic. (Try it!)

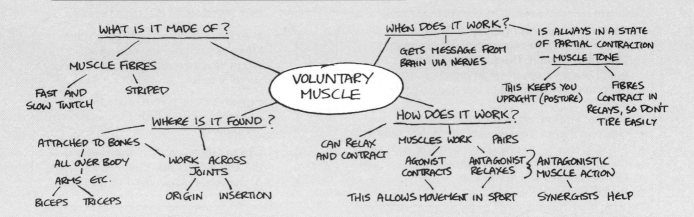

# The different types of exam questions

This page shows you the types of questions used in PE written exams, and gives hints for answering them.

## 1 Multiple choice questions

For these, select the correct letter. If you don't know which is correct, take a guess!

*Example*
Anaerobic respiration produces:
A. glycogen, energy and water.
B. carbon dioxide, water and energy.
C. lactic acid, water and energy.
D. lactic acid and energy.

Answer    *D*

## 2 Short answer questions

You can answer these with a few words or a sentence.

*Example*
(a) What is Knowledge of Performance?
*Information about your performance of a skill or activity.*

(b) Define leisure.
*Leisure is free time when you can do what you want.*

## 3 Longer structured questions

These have several related parts, and you are led through them.

*Example*
(a) Define physical recreation and give an example.
*It is a physical activity you do in your leisure time, for enjoyment. Rollerblading is an example.*

(b) Give **three** benefits to a school leaver of taking part in physical recreation.
1 *It helps to keep you fit.*
2 *It relieves stress and tension.*
3 *You may meet new people and make new friends.*

(c) How do these affect participation in physical recreation?
(i) friends / peer group
*If your friends and peer group enjoy an activity, it will encourage you to participate. If they don't approve of it, that may put you off.*
(ii) facilities
*Facilities encourage participation, especially if they are good, accessible and cheap. People enjoy going there.*

## 4 Open questions

These do not give much help with the answer. It's up to you to show what you know!

*Example*
There are strong links between television and sport. Why are these important?
*The links between TV and sport are important for these reasons:*
*1 TV promotes sport. It gets people interested so they become fans, or take up the sport themselves.*
*It creates sports 'stars' who become role models for young people.*
*2 TV brings money to sport. It pays large sums for broadcast rights to events such as Wimbledon and FA Cup matches. If a sport is shown on TV, it is also easier for the sport to get money from sponsors.*
*3 At the same time sport brings money to TV because it attracts advertising. Companies pay to advertise their goods and services during sports programmes.*
*4 Sport also attracts viewers to TV. Once they're sitting down they may carry on to watch other programmes.*

### Hints on answering open questions
- Look for the instruction word. For example: **Describe, Explain, Discuss, What, Why**. It will point you in the right direction.
- Then make a rough list of key points, or draw a spider map.
- Arrange your points in a logical order.
- Now write your answer, using complete sentences.
- If you give a list of points, introduce it with a colon, as in the last answer above.
- Give examples where you can.
- Add diagrams if they help.

- **Describe** means say what something looks like or how it works. A few words is not enough - you must give some details!

- **Explain** means give reasons for something. Use words like *because* in your answer.

- **Discuss** means look at both sides of the argument. Give the pros and cons, or the advantages and disadvantages.

# And finally, the written exam ...

## A few weeks before the exam
- Start using visualisation. It's a technique athletes use before a big event. Like this ...
- Sit or lie somewhere comfortable, and relax. Close your eyes and spend five minutes imagining yourself in the exam. 'See' yourself reading the paper calmly and answering the questions well.

- Do this every day, up to the exam. It will help you perform well in the exam – as long as you combine it with revision!
- Do it too for your practical test.

## The night before the exam
- Try not to work late.
- Relax before you go to bed. Have a bath, listen to music, watch TV.
- Have an early night. Sleep tight.

## Before you go into the exam
- If you feel nervous, sit somewhere quiet and breathe slowly and deeply for 5 – 10 minutes. This will help to calm you down.

*... I feel calm and relaxed ... I feel calm and relaxed ...*

## In the exam
- Read the instructions calmly and carefully. Note how many questions you must do.
- Read through the whole paper and decide which questions to answer first. It's best to begin with the ones where you feel most confident.
- Then start the questions. Pay special attention to the **instruction** in each question. For example:
  **Give one example...**
  **State two ways ...**
  **Name ...**
  **Define ...**
  **Describe ...**
  **Explain ...**
  Follow the instruction!
- Work as fast as you can, but allow more time for the questions with higher marks. (The marks are shown in brackets after the question.)
- Don't get bogged down in a question. If you get stuck, leave it and try another. You can come back to it later if you have time.
- If you finish early, use the time to check your answers. You can usually gain a few extra marks for good spelling, punctuation and grammar.

And now it's over to you ... GOOD LUCK!

# Health, fitness and exercise

## What is health?
Health is a state of complete physical, mental and social well-being.

### Physical well-being
- ☑ heart, lungs and other body systems working well
- ☑ no illness or injury

### Mental well-being
- ☑ able to cope with stress
- ☑ able to control emotions
- ☑ able to enjoy yourself
- ☑ feelings of self-confidence and self-esteem

### Social well-being
- ☑ enough food, clothing and shelter
- ☑ friends and support
- ☑ a belief you have some value in society (school, family, job)

### All three affect each other.
- Falling ill may affect your mental and social well-being.
- Losing your job may affect your physical and mental well-being.

## What is fitness?
Fitness is the ability to meet the demands of the environment.

do your school work

do your homework

tidy your room

go shopping for clothes

do what you're told

pull up your socks

stick with that job in the garden centre

practice the trombone

get good at maths

party on Saturday

If you can carry out all your tasks and activities *without getting too tired*, and still have energy left over for emergencies, you are fit.

## What is exercise?
Exercise is an activity you do to improve your health and fitness. It is the link between them.

health

exercise improves health

exercise makes you fitter

fitness

## Fitness is relative
- Demands are different for everyone.
- So everyone does not need the same level of fitness.
- The important thing is to be able to meet the demands on *you*.

increasing level of fitness

## A healthy lifestyle
A healthy lifestyle means a way of life that promotes good health. It includes ...

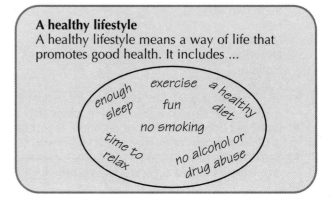

enough sleep   exercise   a healthy diet   fun   no smoking   time to relax   no alcohol or drug abuse

Q1, page 79 ▷

# Exercise and the body systems

All your **body systems** work together, to help you exercise.

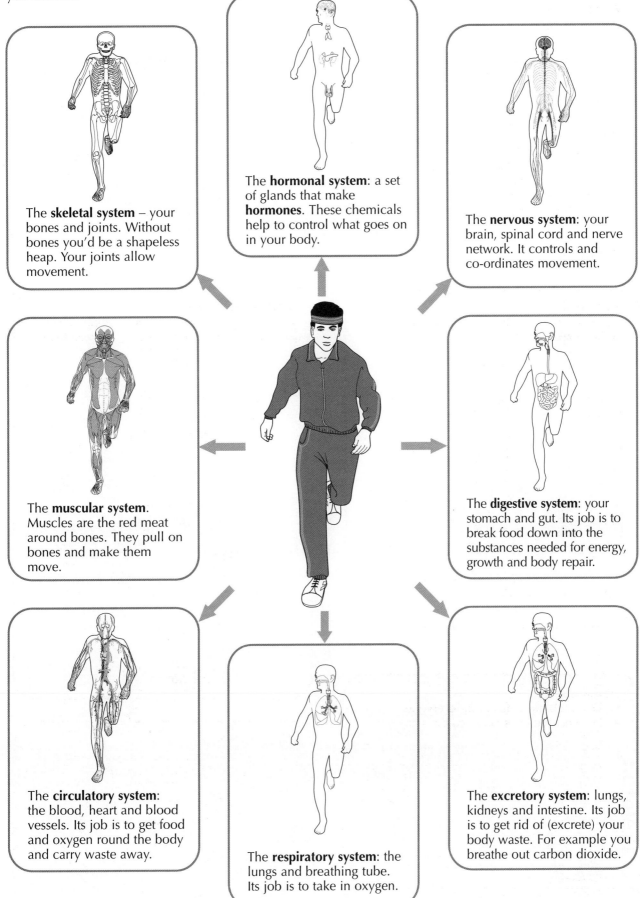

The **skeletal system** – your bones and joints. Without bones you'd be a shapeless heap. Your joints allow movement.

The **hormonal system**: a set of glands that make **hormones**. These chemicals help to control what goes on in your body.

The **nervous system**: your brain, spinal cord and nerve network. It controls and co-ordinates movement.

The **muscular system**. Muscles are the red meat around bones. They pull on bones and make them move.

The **digestive system**: your stomach and gut. Its job is to break food down into the substances needed for energy, growth and body repair.

The **circulatory system**: the blood, heart and blood vessels. Its job is to get food and oxygen round the body and carry waste away.

The **respiratory system**: the lungs and breathing tube. Its job is to take in oxygen.

The **excretory system**: lungs, kidneys and intestine. Its job is to get rid of (excrete) your body waste. For example you breathe out carbon dioxide.

Q2, page 79

# The skeleton

Your skeleton is made up of **bones**, held together at **joints**. These are its main bones:

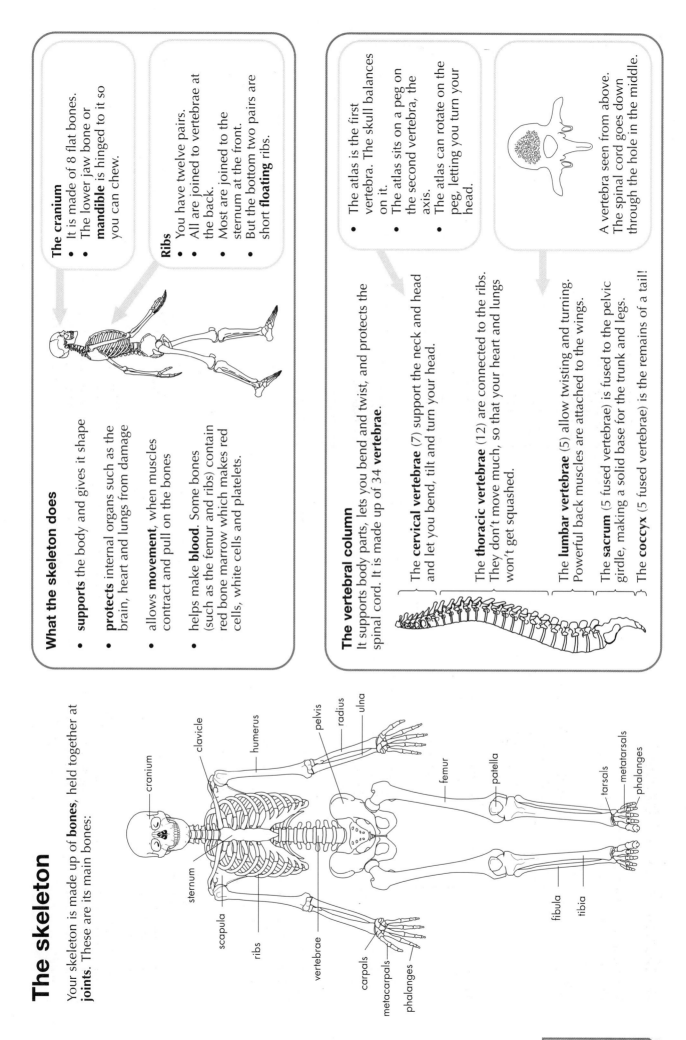

## What the skeleton does

- **supports** the body and gives it shape

- **protects** internal organs such as the brain, heart and lungs from damage

- allows **movement**, when muscles contract and pull on the bones

- helps make **blood**. Some bones (such as the femur and ribs) contain red bone marrow which makes red cells, white cells and platelets.

## The vertebral column

It supports body parts, lets you bend and twist, and protects the spinal cord. It is made up of 34 **vertebrae.**

The **cervical vertebrae** (7) support the neck and head and let you bend, tilt and turn your head.

The **thoracic vertebrae** (12) are connected to the ribs. They don't move much, so that your heart and lungs won't get squashed.

The **lumbar vertebrae** (5) allow twisting and turning. Powerful back muscles are attached to the wings.

The **sacrum** (5 fused vertebrae) is fused to the pelvic girdle, making a solid base for the trunk and legs.

The **coccyx** (5 fused vertebrae) is the remains of a tail!

### The cranium

- It is made of 8 flat bones.
- The lower jaw bone or **mandible** is hinged to it so you can chew.

### Ribs

- You have twelve pairs.
- All are joined to vertebrae at the back.
- Most are joined to the sternum at the front.
- But the bottom two pairs are short **floating** ribs.

- The atlas is the first vertebra. The skull balances on it.
- The atlas sits on a peg on the second vertebra, the axis.
- The atlas can rotate on the peg, letting you turn your head.

A vertebra seen from above. The spinal cord goes down through the hole in the middle.

Q3 and 4, page 79 ▶

# A closer look at bones

## A typical adult long bone
The arm and leg bones of an adult look like this:

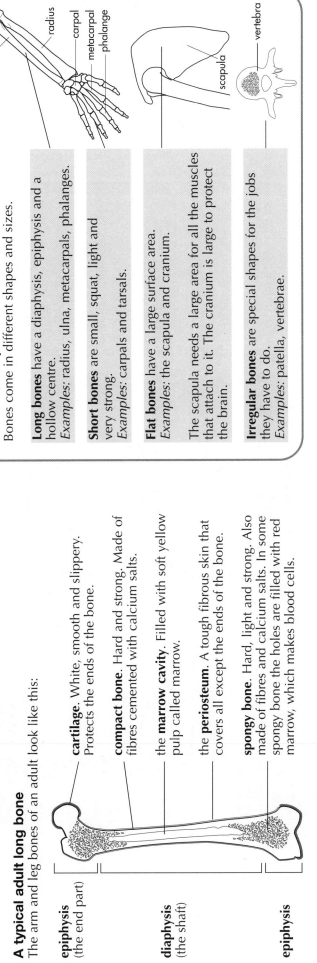

epiphysis (the end part)

diaphysis (the shaft)

epiphysis

**cartilage.** White, smooth and slippery. Protects the ends of the bone.

**compact bone.** Hard and strong. Made of fibres cemented with calcium salts.

the **marrow cavity.** Filled with soft yellow pulp called marrow.

the **periosteum.** A tough fibrous skin that covers all except the ends of the bone.

**spongy bone.** Hard, light and strong. Also made of fibres and calcium salts. In some spongy bone the holes are filled with red marrow, which makes blood cells.

## Different shapes of bones
Bones come in different shapes and sizes.

**Long bones** have a diaphysis, epiphysis and a hollow centre.
*Examples*: radius, ulna, metacarpals, phalanges.

**Short bones** are small, squat, light and very strong.
*Examples*: carpals and tarsals.

**Flat bones** have a large surface area.
*Examples*: the scapula and cranium.

The scapula needs a large area for all the muscles that attach to it. The cranium is large to protect the brain.

**Irregular bones** are special shapes for the jobs they have to do.
*Examples*: patella, vertebrae.

ulna — radius — carpal — metacarpal — phalange

scapula

vertebra

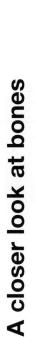

Q5, page 79

# How bones grow
Inside the womb, bones start life as **cartilage.**
Over the years this turns into bone in a process called **ossification.**

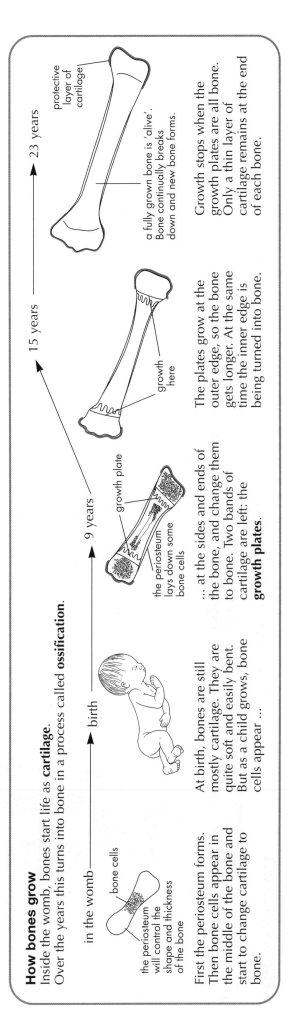

in the womb → birth → 9 years → 15 years → 23 years

bone cells

the periosteum will control the shape and thickness of the bone

First the periosteum forms. Then bone cells appear in the middle of the bone and start to change cartilage to bone.

At birth, bones are still mostly cartilage. They are quite soft and easily bent. But as a child grows, bone cells appear ...

growth plate

the periosteum lays down some bone cells

... at the sides and ends of the bone, and change them to bone. Two bands of cartilage are left: the **growth plates.**

growth here

The plates grow at the outer edge, so the bone gets longer. At the same time the inner edge is being turned into bone.

protective layer of cartilage

a fully grown bone is 'alive'. Bone continually breaks down and new bone forms.

Growth stops when the growth plates are all bone. Only a thin layer of cartilage remains at the end of each bone.

# Joints

Joints are where bones meet. There are three types...

## Fixed or immovable joints

The bones at an immovable joint can't move. They interlock or overlap, and are held together by tough fibre.
*Example:* the joints between plates in the cranium.

fixed joint — tough fibre — bone

## Slightly movable joints

The bones at a slightly movable joint can move only a little. They are held together by straps called **ligaments** and joined by pads of gristly **cartilage**.
*Example:* the joints between most vertebrae.

vertebrae — pad of cartilage

ligaments — cartilage — bone

The pads of cartilage act as shock absorbers so the bones won't jar when you run and jump.

## Freely movable joints

At freely movable joints, the bones can move quite freely. These joints are also called **synovial joints**.
*Examples:* the shoulder, elbow, hip, knee and ankle joints.

## The knee joint: a typical freely movable joint

bone — joint cavity filled with synovial fluid — cartilage

ligament — joint capsule — synovial membrane

A freely movable joint has these parts:

- an outer sleeve or **joint capsule**. It helps to hold the bones in place and protects the joint. It is a continuation of the periosteum on each bone.
- a **synovial membrane**. It is the capsule lining. It oozes a slippery liquid called **synovial fluid**.
- a **joint cavity**. This is the gap between the bones. It is filled with synovial fluid, which lubricates the joint so that the bones can move more easily.
- a covering of smooth slippery **cartilage** on the ends of the bones, to stop them knocking together.
- **ligaments** to hold the bones together and keep them in place.

### Cartilage

- protects bones and stops them knocking together.
- forms a gristly cushion between bones at slightly movable joints (for example between vertebrae).
- forms a smooth slippery coat on the ends of bones at freely movable joints.

### Ligaments

- are strong cords and straps that lash bones together.
- hold a joint in place.
- are slightly elastic, just enough to let the bones move the way they should.

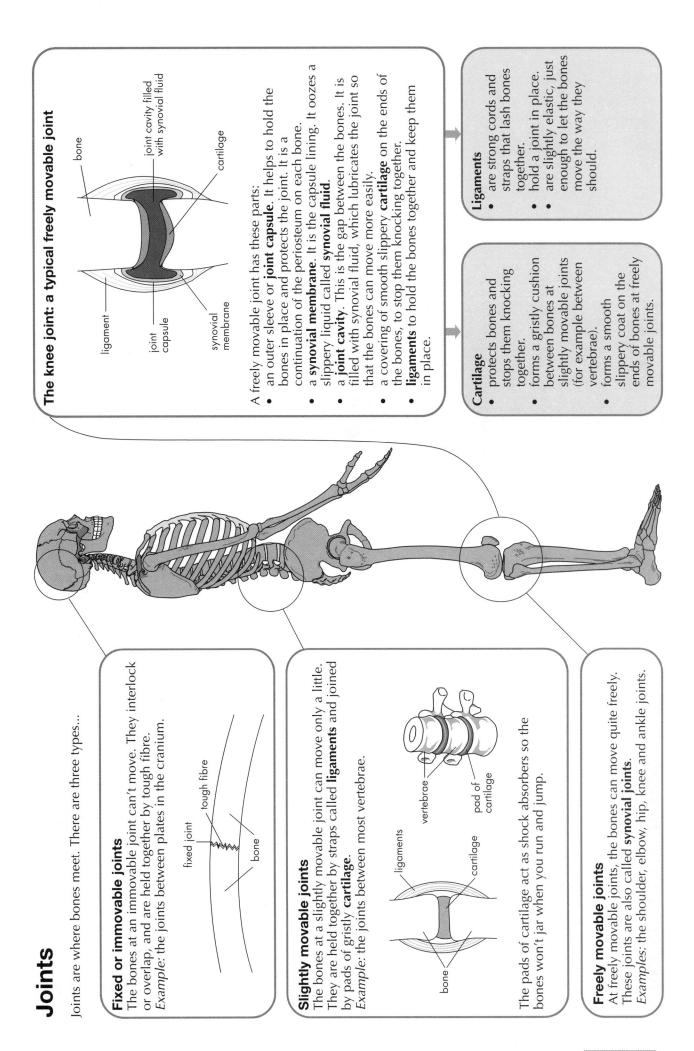

Q6, page 79

# More about freely movable joints

## Types of freely movable joints

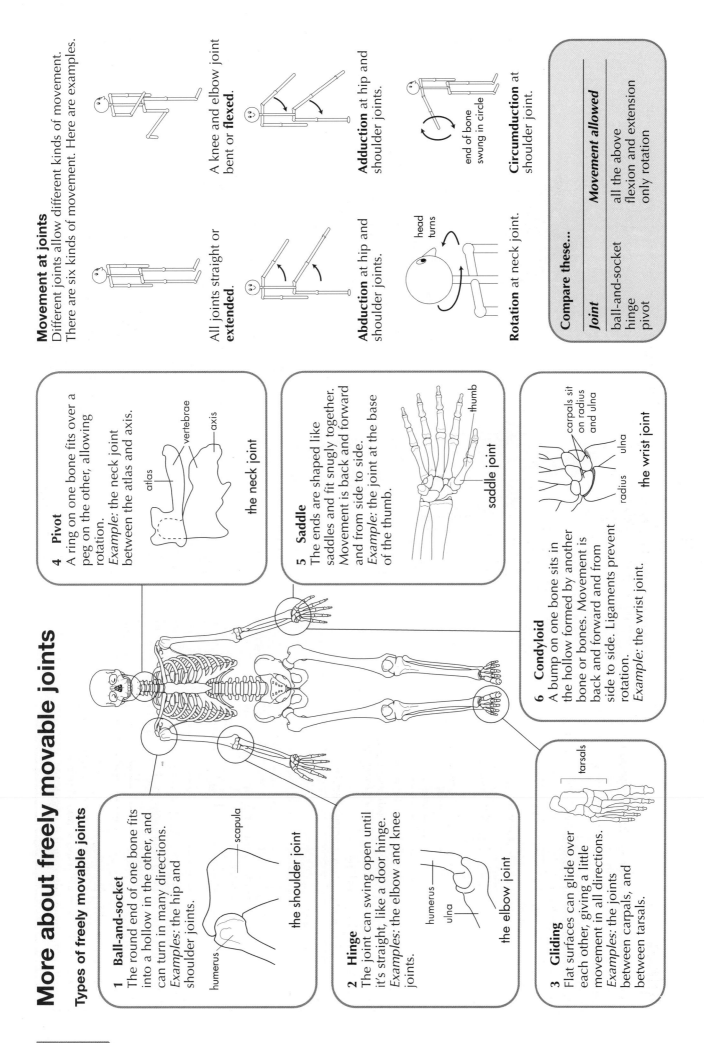

**1  Ball-and-socket**
The round end of one bone fits into a hollow in the other, and can turn in many directions.
*Examples:* the hip and shoulder joints.

humerus — scapula

the shoulder joint

**2  Hinge**
The joint can swing open until it's straight, like a door hinge.
*Examples:* the elbow and knee joints.

humerus — ulna

the elbow joint

**3  Gliding**
Flat surfaces can glide over each other, giving a little movement in all directions.
*Examples:* the joints between carpals, and between tarsals.

tarsals

**4  Pivot**
A ring on one bone fits over a peg on the other, allowing rotation.
*Example:* the neck joint between the atlas and axis.

atlas — vertebrae — axis

the neck joint

**5  Saddle**
The ends are shaped like saddles and fit snugly together. Movement is back and forward and from side to side.
*Example:* the joint at the base of the thumb.

thumb

saddle joint

**6  Condyloid**
A bump on one bone sits in the hollow formed by another bone or bones. Movement is back and forward and from side to side. Ligaments prevent rotation.
*Example:* the wrist joint.

carpals sit on radius and ulna — ulna — radius

the wrist joint

## Movement at joints
Different joints allow different kinds of movement. There are six kinds of movement. Here are examples.

A knee and elbow joint bent or **flexed**.

All joints straight or **extended**.

**Adduction** at hip and shoulder joints.

**Abduction** at hip and shoulder joints.

end of bone swung in circle
**Circumduction** at shoulder joint.

head turns
**Rotation** at neck joint.

**Compare these...**

| Joint | Movement allowed |
|---|---|
| ball-and-socket | all the above |
| hinge | flexion and extension |
| pivot | only rotation |

Q7, page 79

# Muscles

Every movement that takes place in your body depends on muscles. They work by **shortening** or **contracting**.

## The three kinds of muscle

### 1 Involuntary
- Works away without you thinking about it.
- Also called **smooth**.
- Found in the walls of inner organs such as arteries, stomach and gut.

When the muscle in artery walls contracts it squirts blood along.

blood →

When the muscle in gut walls contracts it pushes food along.

food →

### 2 Voluntary
- Attached to bones. (It's the red meat on bones.)
- Works when you want it to, for example when you decide to run or jump.
- Also called **striped** and **skeletal**.

### 3 Cardiac
- Forms the walls of your heart.
- Works non-stop all through life.
- It is involuntary *and* striped.
- Has its own blood supply.

When it contracts it pumps blood out of the heart and round the body.

## The main voluntary muscles in your body

The muscles that move your bones when you exercise are voluntary muscles. These are the main ones.

5 pectoral

1 deltoid

2 biceps

3 abdominals

4 quadriceps

7 trapezius

8 triceps

9 gluteals

gluteus maximus

11 gastrocnemius

6 latissimus dorsi

10 hamstrings

| Muscle(s) | Main action(s) |
|---|---|
| 1 deltoids (3 muscles) | Raise your arm forwards, backward and sideways at the shoulder. |
| 2 biceps | Bends your arm at the elbow. |
| 3 abdominals (4 muscles) | Pull in the abdomen. Flex the spine so you can bend forward. |
| 4 quadriceps (4 muscles) | Straighten the leg at the knee. Keep it straight when you stand. |
| 5 pectorals (2 muscles) | Raise your arm at the shoulder. Draw it across your chest. |
| 6 latissimus dorsi (lats) | Pull your arm down at the shoulder. Draw it behind your back. |
| 7 trapezius | Holds and rotates your shoulders. Moves your head back and sideways. |
| 8 triceps | Straightens your arm at the elbow joint. |
| 9 gluteals (3 muscles) | Pull your leg back at the hip. Raise it sideways at the hip. Gluteus maximus is the biggest of these muscles. |
| 10 hamstrings (3 muscles) | Bend your leg at the knee. |
| 11 gastrocnemius | Straightens the ankle joint so you can stand on your tiptoes. |

Q8, page 79

# A closer look at voluntary muscle

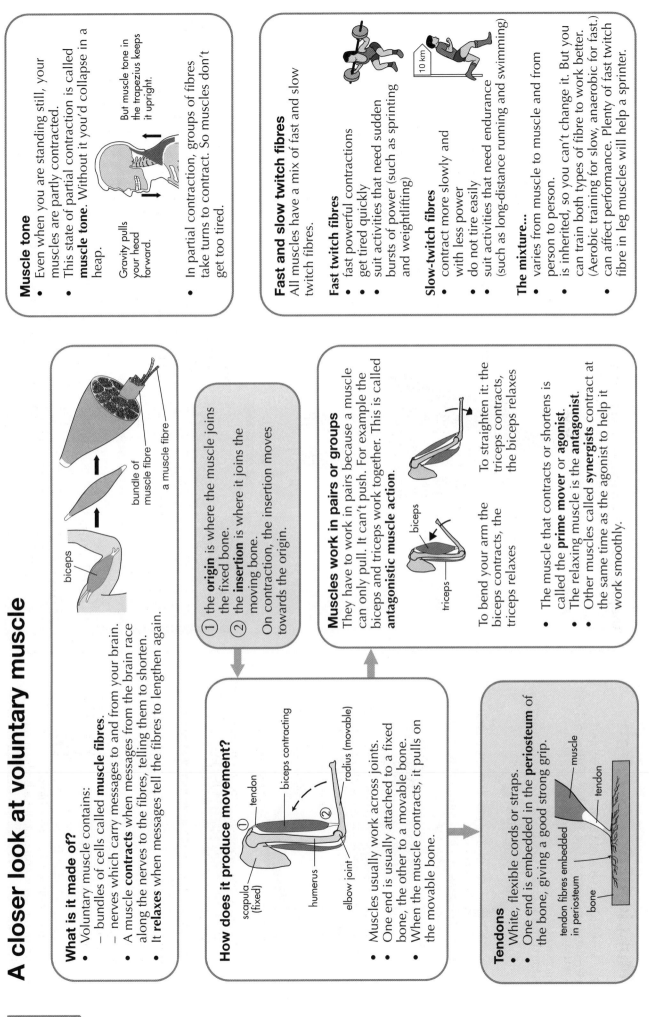

## What is it made of?

- Voluntary muscle contains:
  - bundles of cells called **muscle fibres.**
  - nerves which carry messages to and from your brain.
- A muscle **contracts** when messages from the brain race along the nerves to the fibres, telling them to shorten.
- It **relaxes** when messages tell the fibres to lengthen again.

biceps

bundle of
muscle fibre
a muscle fibre

## How does it produce movement?

① the **origin** is where the muscle joins the fixed bone.
② the **insertion** is where it joins the moving bone.
On contraction, the insertion moves towards the origin.

scapula (fixed)
① tendon
biceps contracting
radius (movable)
humerus
elbow joint
②

- Muscles usually work across joints.
- One end is usually attached to a fixed bone, the other to a movable bone.
- When the muscle contracts, it pulls on the movable bone.

## Muscles work in pairs or groups

They have to work in pairs because a muscle can only pull. It can't push. For example the biceps and triceps work together. This is called **antagonistic muscle action.**

biceps
triceps

To bend your arm the biceps contracts, the triceps relaxes

To straighten it: the triceps contracts, the biceps relaxes

- The muscle that contracts or shortens is called the **prime mover** or **agonist.**
- The relaxing muscle is the **antagonist.**
- Other muscles called **synergists** contract at the same time as the agonist to help it work smoothly.

## Tendons

- White, flexible cords or straps.
- One end is embedded in the **periosteum** of the bone, giving a good strong grip.

muscle
tendon
tendon fibres embedded in periosteum
bone

## Muscle tone

- Even when you are standing still, your muscles are partly contracted.
- This state of partial contraction is called **muscle tone**. Without it you'd collapse in a heap.

Gravity pulls your head forward.
But muscle tone in the trapezius keeps it upright.

- In partial contraction, groups of fibres take turns to contract. So muscles don't get too tired.

## Fast and slow twitch fibres

All muscles have a mix of fast and slow twitch fibres.

**Fast twitch fibres**
- fast powerful contractions
- get tired quickly
- suit activities that need sudden bursts of power (such as sprinting and weightlifting)

**Slow-twitch fibres**
- contract more slowly and with less power
- do not tire easily
- suit activities that need endurance (such as long-distance running and swimming)

10 km

**The mixture…**
- varies from muscle to muscle and from person to person.
- is inherited, so you can't change it. But you can train both types of fibre to work better. (Aerobic training for slow, anaerobic for fast.)
- can affect performance. Plenty of fast twitch fibre in leg muscles will help a sprinter.

Q9, page 80

# The circulatory system

The heart, blood vessels and blood form the **circulatory system**. Its job is to move oxygen, food and other substances around the body. Here is a simple plan of it.

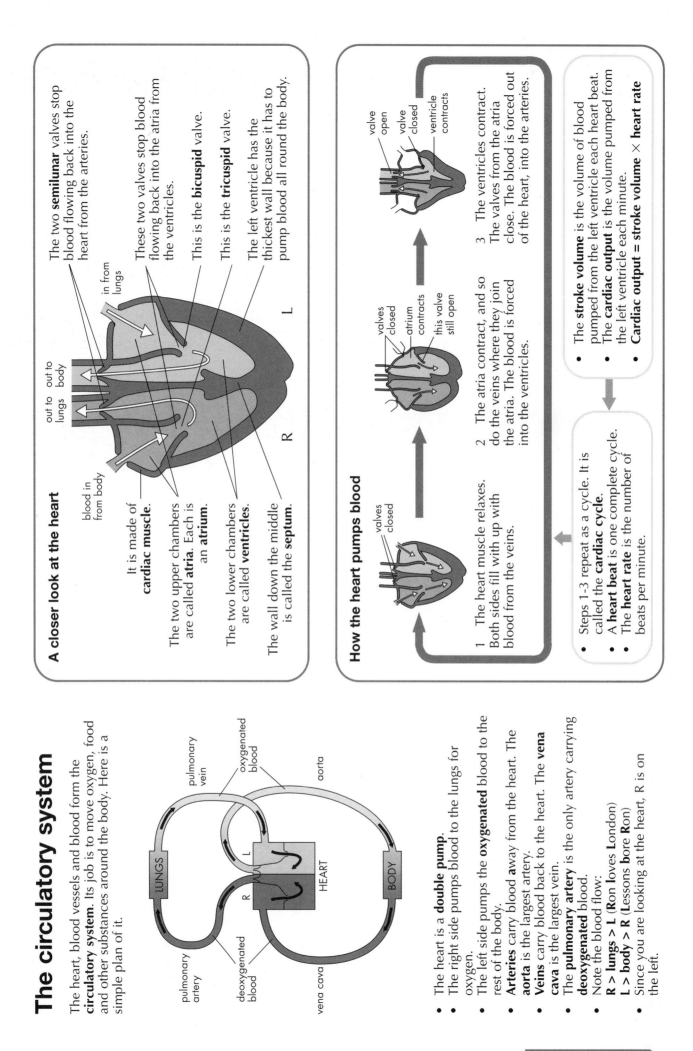

pulmonary vein

oxygenated blood

pulmonary artery

deoxygenated blood

aorta

LUNGS

L

R

HEART

BODY

vena cava

- The heart is a **double pump**.
- The right side pumps blood to the lungs for oxygen.
- The left side pumps the **oxygenated** blood to the rest of the body.
- **Arteries** carry blood **away** from the heart. The **aorta** is the largest artery.
- **Veins** carry blood **back** to the heart. The **vena cava** is the largest vein.
- The **pulmonary artery** is the only artery carrying **deoxygenated** blood.
- Note the blood flow:
- **R > lungs > L** (Ron loves London)
- **L > body > R** (Lessons bore Ron)
- Since you are looking at the heart, R is on the left.

## A closer look at the heart

The two **semilunar** valves stop blood flowing back into the heart from the arteries.

These two valves stop blood flowing back into the atria from the ventricles.

This is the **bicuspid** valve.

This is the **tricuspid** valve.

The left ventricle has the thickest wall because it has to pump blood all round the body.

in from lungs

out to lungs

out to body

blood in from body

L

R

It is made of **cardiac muscle.**

The two upper chambers are called **atria**. Each is an **atrium**.

The two lower chambers are called **ventricles**.

The wall down the middle is called the **septum**.

## How the heart pumps blood

valves closed

valves closed

atrium contracts

this valve still open

valve open

valve closed

ventricle contracts

1  The heart muscle relaxes. Both sides fill with up with blood from the veins.

2  The atria contract, and so do the veins where they join the atria. The blood is forced into the ventricles.

3  The ventricles contract. The valves from the atria close. The blood is forced out of the heart, into the arteries.

Steps 1-3 repeat as a cycle. It is called the **cardiac cycle.**

- A **heart beat** is one complete cycle.
- The **heart rate** is the number of beats per minute.

- The **stroke volume** is the volume of blood pumped from the left ventricle each heart beat.
- The **cardiac output** is the volume pumped from the left ventricle each minute.
- **Cardiac output = stroke volume × heart rate**

Q10 and 11, page 80

# A closer look at blood

## How blood is carried round the body

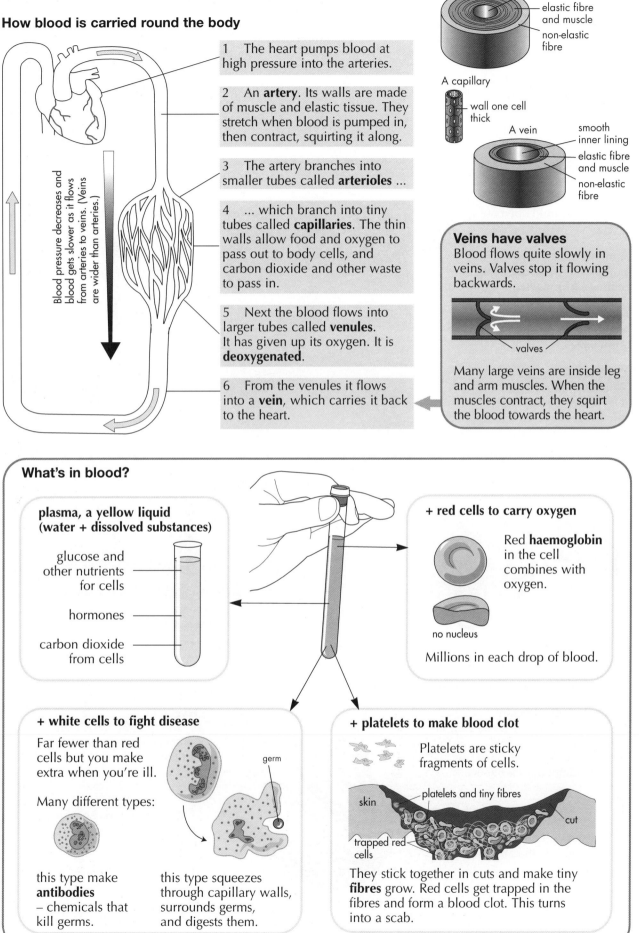

Blood pressure decreases and blood gets slower as it flows from arteries to veins. (Veins are wider than arteries.)

1  The heart pumps blood at high pressure into the arteries.

2  An **artery**. Its walls are made of muscle and elastic tissue. They stretch when blood is pumped in, then contract, squirting it along.

3  The artery branches into smaller tubes called **arterioles** ...

4  ... which branch into tiny tubes called **capillaries**. The thin walls allow food and oxygen to pass out to body cells, and carbon dioxide and other waste to pass in.

5  Next the blood flows into larger tubes called **venules**. It has given up its oxygen. It is **deoxygenated**.

6  From the venules it flows into a **vein**, which carries it back to the heart.

An artery — smooth inner lining, elastic fibre and muscle, non-elastic fibre

A capillary — wall one cell thick

A vein — smooth inner lining, elastic fibre and muscle, non-elastic fibre

### Veins have valves
Blood flows quite slowly in veins. Valves stop it flowing backwards.

valves

Many large veins are inside leg and arm muscles. When the muscles contract, they squirt the blood towards the heart.

## What's in blood?

**plasma, a yellow liquid (water + dissolved substances)**

glucose and other nutrients for cells

hormones

carbon dioxide from cells

**+ red cells to carry oxygen**

Red **haemoglobin** in the cell combines with oxygen.

no nucleus

Millions in each drop of blood.

**+ white cells to fight disease**

Far fewer than red cells but you make extra when you're ill.

Many different types:

germ

this type make **antibodies** – chemicals that kill germs.

this type squeezes through capillary walls, surrounds germs, and digests them.

**+ platelets to make blood clot**

Platelets are sticky fragments of cells.

skin

platelets and tiny fibres

cut

trapped red cells

They stick together in cuts and make tiny **fibres** grow. Red cells get trapped in the fibres and form a blood clot. This turns into a scab.

Q12, page 80

# The respiratory system and gas exchange

### The respiratory system
- The nose, lungs and breathing tubes form the **respiratory system**.
- Its job is to take in oxygen for the body cells, and get rid of carbon dioxide.

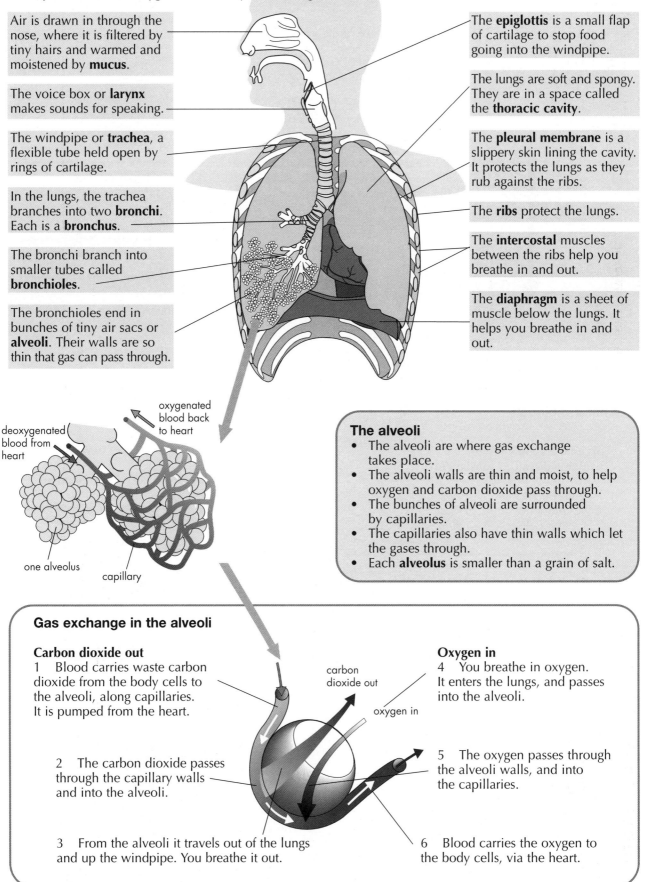

Air is drawn in through the nose, where it is filtered by tiny hairs and warmed and moistened by **mucus**.

The voice box or **larynx** makes sounds for speaking.

The windpipe or **trachea**, a flexible tube held open by rings of cartilage.

In the lungs, the trachea branches into two **bronchi**. Each is a **bronchus**.

The bronchi branch into smaller tubes called **bronchioles**.

The bronchioles end in bunches of tiny air sacs or **alveoli**. Their walls are so thin that gas can pass through.

The **epiglottis** is a small flap of cartilage to stop food going into the windpipe.

The lungs are soft and spongy. They are in a space called the **thoracic cavity**.

The **pleural membrane** is a slippery skin lining the cavity. It protects the lungs as they rub against the ribs.

The **ribs** protect the lungs.

The **intercostal** muscles between the ribs help you breathe in and out.

The **diaphragm** is a sheet of muscle below the lungs. It helps you breathe in and out.

oxygenated blood back to heart

deoxygenated blood from heart

one alveolus

capillary

### The alveoli
- The alveoli are where gas exchange takes place.
- The alveoli walls are thin and moist, to help oxygen and carbon dioxide pass through.
- The bunches of alveoli are surrounded by capillaries.
- The capillaries also have thin walls which let the gases through.
- Each **alveolus** is smaller than a grain of salt.

### Gas exchange in the alveoli

**Carbon dioxide out**
1   Blood carries waste carbon dioxide from the body cells to the alveoli, along capillaries. It is pumped from the heart.

2   The carbon dioxide passes through the capillary walls and into the alveoli.

3   From the alveoli it travels out of the lungs and up the windpipe. You breathe it out.

carbon dioxide out

oxygen in

**Oxygen in**
4   You breathe in oxygen. It enters the lungs, and passes into the alveoli.

5   The oxygen passes through the alveoli walls, and into the capillaries.

6   Blood carries the oxygen to the body cells, via the heart.

**14**   Part one: The body

Q13, page 80

# A closer look at breathing

Breathing is your way of taking in oxygen and getting rid of carbon dioxide. It is also called **respiration**. Don't confuse it with respiration in cells!

- Breathing in is also called **inhaling**.
- Breathing out is **exhaling**.

## When you breathe in

1 The intercostal muscles contract. This pulls the rib cage upwards. So the chest expands.

2 The diaphragm contracts. This pulls it down and flattens it, making the chest even larger.

3 The lungs expand too, because their moist surface clings to the chest lining.

4 So air is sucked down the windpipe and into the lungs.

## When you breathe out

The opposite changes take place.

1 The intercostal muscles relax. This lowers the rib cage and makes the chest smaller.

2 The diaphragm relaxes so it bulges upwards again. This makes the chest even smaller.

3 So the lungs get compressed, forcing air out and up the windpipe.

## How air changes in your lungs

Air *in*
- about 21% oxygen
- about 79% nitrogen
- a tiny amount of carbon dioxide
- a little water vapour

*At this very moment, my billions of cells are using oxygen to get energy, and giving out carbon dioxide and water vapour...*

Air *out*
- about 17% oxygen,
- about 79% nitrogen
- 3% carbon dioxide
- a lot of water vapour

## How much air do you breathe?

- The **tidal volume** is the volume of air you breathe in (or out) with each breath.
- The **respiratory rate** is the number of breaths you take per minute.
- The **minute volume** is the volume of air you breathe in per minute. All three increase during exercise.

For a typical 18-year-old

|  | | |
|---|---|---|
| TV (litres) | 0.5 | 2.5 |
| RR (breaths/min) | 12 | 30 |
| MV (litres/min) | 6 | 75 |

**Minute volume = tidal volume × respiratory rate**

## How big are your lungs?

- The **vital capacity** is the maximum volume of air you can breathe out, after breathing in as deeply as you can. (Usually around 4.5 or 5 litres.)
- Training increases your vital capacity.
- The **residual volume** is the amount of air left in your lungs after you breathe out as hard as you can. (Usually around 1.5 litres.) You can never empty your lungs completely.

vital capacity

residual volume

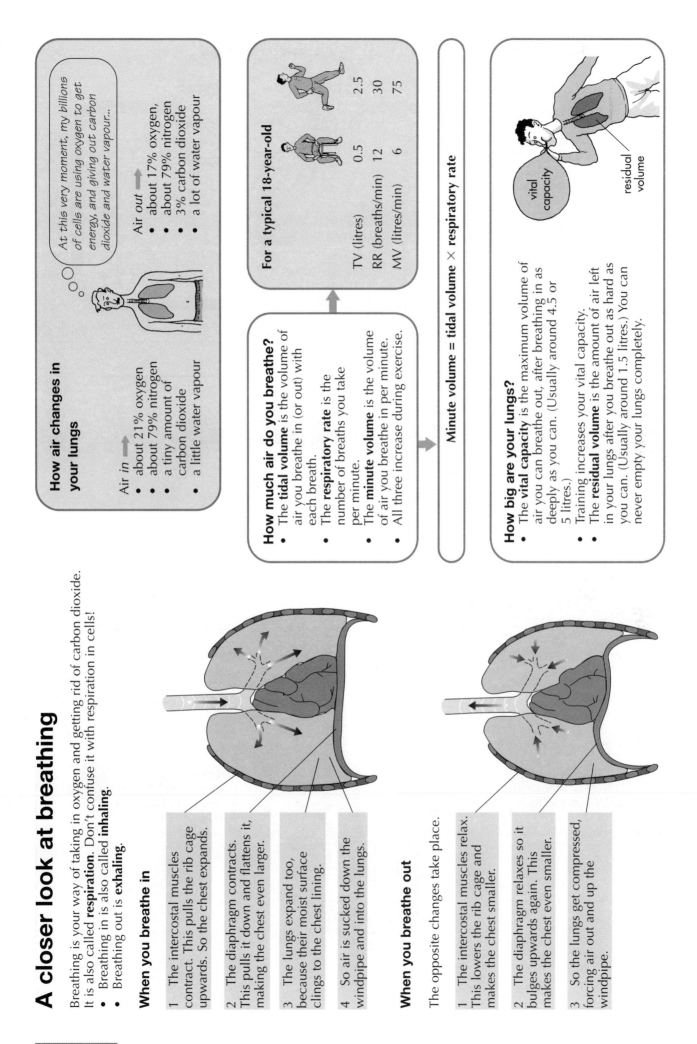

Q14, page 80

# Energy for exercise

You can walk and run and jump because muscles **contract**. This needs **energy**.

glucose + oxygen → muscle → energy for contraction

Muscles get most of their energy from their reaction between **glucose** and **oxygen**.

**Glucose** is obtained from food, and carried from the digestive system by blood.

**Oxygen** is obtained from the air, and carried from the lungs by blood.

## How oxygen reaches the muscles

1  Blood is pumped to the lungs to pick up oxygen.

2  The oxygen joins with the haemoglobin in red cells to form **oxyhaemoglobin**. This is bright red.

3  The **oxygenated** blood is pumped round the body.

4  In the capillaries, oxyhaemoglobin breaks down, and oxygen is set free.

5  The oxygen passes out to the muscle fibres and other body cells.

6  The blood is now dull red – it is **deoxygenated**. It needs to collect more oxygen. Back to step 1.

## How glucose reaches the muscles

In your digestive system, glucose is obtained from **carbohydrates**. These are found in foods such as pasta, rice, potatoes and bread.

part of a starch molecule

glucose molecules

1  Starch is a carbohydrate found in rice and pasta. It is a string of glucose molecules joined together.

2  During digestion, enzymes break starch down into glucose.

3  The glucose passes out through the gut walls and into the blood stream, to be carried round the body.

blood stream

4  Some gets stored in the **muscles** as **glycogen**. This breaks down again during exercise.

muscles

5  Some gets stored in the **liver** as **glycogen**, and released again when the glucose level in the blood falls too low.

liver

6  The rest is carried to all the other cells of the body.

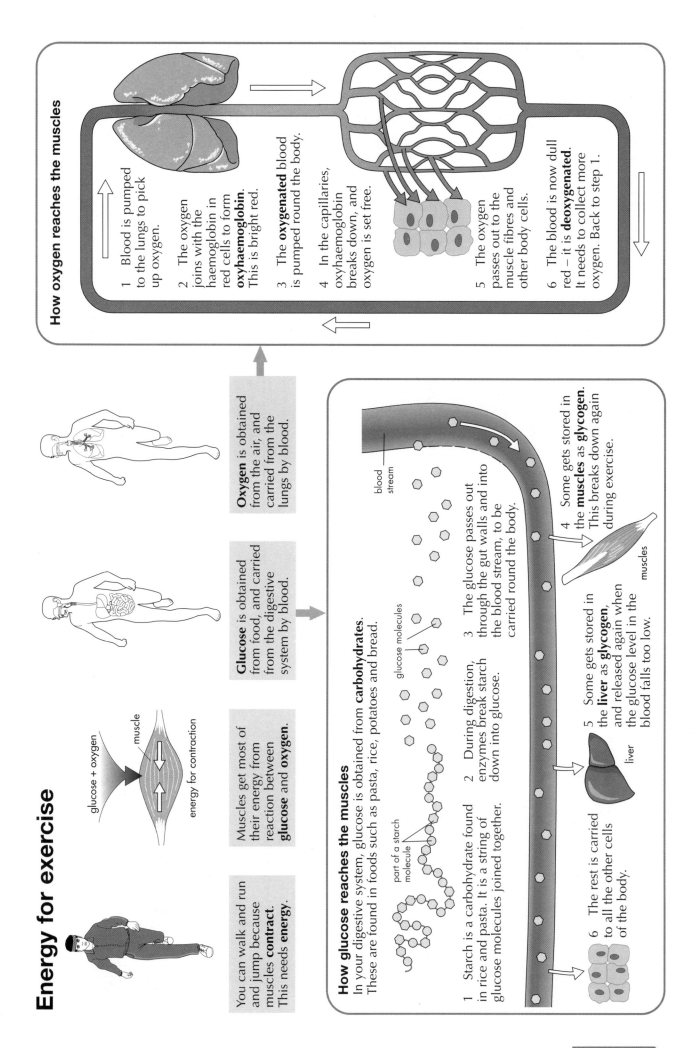

Q15, page 80

# The reactions that provide muscles with energy

- In muscle fibres (and other body cells) energy is obtained from glucose.
- When this process uses oxygen, it is called **aerobic respiration**.
- When it does *not* use oxygen, it is called **anaerobic respiration**.

### Aerobic respiration
Most of the time your muscles depend on aerobic respiration.

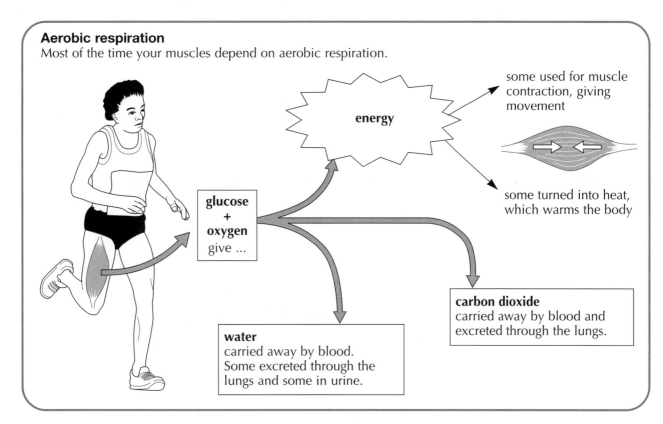

energy

some used for muscle contraction, giving movement

some turned into heat, which warms the body

**glucose + oxygen** give ...

**carbon dioxide**
carried away by blood and excreted through the lungs.

**water**
carried away by blood. Some excreted through the lungs and some in urine.

### Anaerobic respiration
- During all-out effort such as sprinting, muscles need a lot of energy fast.
- But oxygen can't reach the muscles fast enough.
- So anaerobic respiration takes over.

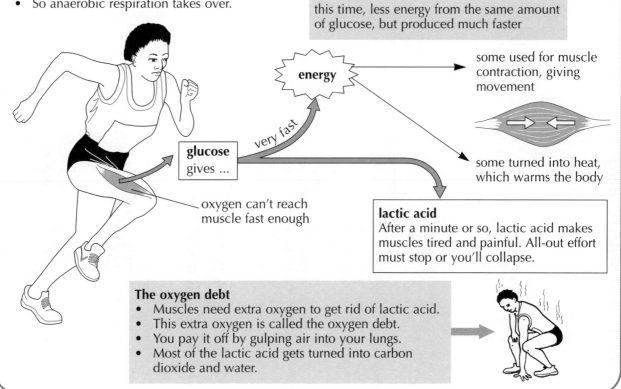

this time, less energy from the same amount of glucose, but produced much faster

energy

some used for muscle contraction, giving movement

some turned into heat, which warms the body

**glucose** gives ...

very fast

oxygen can't reach muscle fast enough

**lactic acid**
After a minute or so, lactic acid makes muscles tired and painful. All-out effort must stop or you'll collapse.

**The oxygen debt**
- Muscles need extra oxygen to get rid of lactic acid.
- This extra oxygen is called the oxygen debt.
- You pay it off by gulping air into your lungs.
- Most of the lactic acid gets turned into carbon dioxide and water.

Q16, page 81

# How the body changes during exercise

Many changes take place in your body during exercise, or when you're playing a sport.

1 First, the muscles start to work harder. So respiration speeds up in muscle fibres to provide the extra energy.

2 This means more carbon dioxide forms. The level rises in your blood.

3 The brain detects this rise. It sends signals to your heart and lungs to work faster.

4 The lungs start breathing faster and more deeply. They remove carbon dioxide faster and take in oxygen faster.

5 At the same time the heart starts beating faster, pumping blood faster around the body.

6 Meanwhile, contracting muscles squeeze on veins, squirting blood faster back to the heart.

7 So the heart fills up fuller when it relaxes. This stretches it like elastic, so it contracts more strongly. It pumps out more blood at each beat.

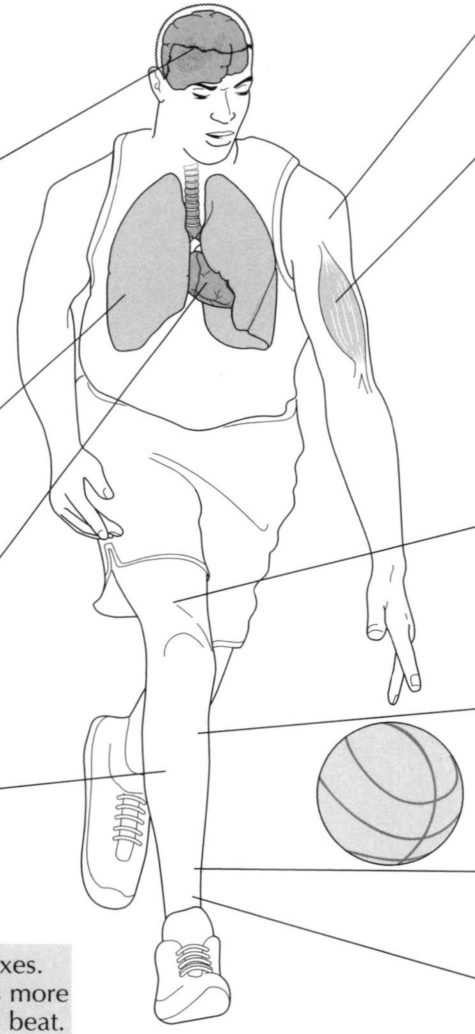

8 Since the heart and lungs are both working harder, more oxygen reaches the muscles each minute, and more carbon dioxide is carried away.

9 This means the muscles can keep on working hard.

Note these changes too:

10 Arterioles widen so that the blood pressure won't get too high.

11 Blood gets shunted from where it is needed less, to where the action is. For example from the gut to the legs. (To make this happen, blood vessels widen and constrict at different points – **vasodilation** and **vasoconstriction**.)

12 The increased respiration in the muscles generates more heat. So your blood gets hotter.

13 To cool the blood down, more is shunted close to the skin. This makes your skin redden.

14 You also sweat, which cools you by evaporation.

## Summary of the changes

Respiration in the muscles increases, to provide energy for contractions.

This means more oxygen is needed and more carbon dioxide formed.

So the heart-lung team works harder to cope.

Changes also take place to shunt more blood to where it's needed, keep it cool, and keep its pressure down.

heart rate
stroke volume
cardiac output
blood pressure

respiratory rate
tidal volume
minute volume

all these increase during exercise

Q17, page 81

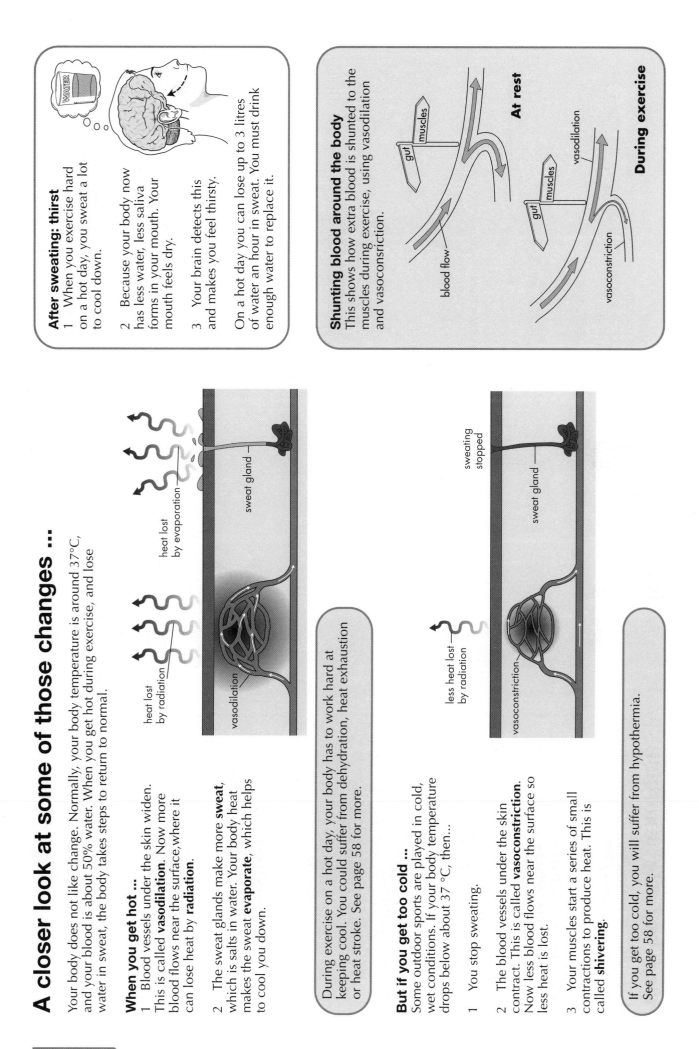

# A closer look at some of those changes ...

Your body does not like change. Normally, your body temperature is around 37°C, and your blood is about 50% water. When you get hot during exercise, and lose water in sweat, the body takes steps to return to normal.

## When you get hot ...

1  Blood vessels under the skin widen. This is called **vasodilation**. Now more blood flows near the surface, where it can lose heat by **radiation**.

2  The sweat glands make more **sweat**, which is salts in water. Your body heat makes the sweat **evaporate**, which helps to cool you down.

heat lost by radiation

heat lost by evaporation

vasodilation

sweat gland

During exercise on a hot day, your body has to work hard at keeping cool. You could suffer from dehydration, heat exhaustion or heat stroke. See page 58 for more.

## But if you get too cold ...

Some outdoor sports are played in cold, wet conditions. If your body temperature drops below about 37 °C, then...

1  You stop sweating.

2  The blood vessels under the skin contract. This is called **vasoconstriction**. Now less blood flows near the surface so less heat is lost.

3  Your muscles start a series of small contractions to produce heat. This is called **shivering**.

If you get too cold, you will suffer from hypothermia. See page 58 for more.

less heat lost by radiation

vasoconstriction

sweating stopped

sweat gland

## After sweating: thirst

1  When you exercise hard on a hot day, you sweat a lot to cool down.

2  Because your body now has less water, less saliva forms in your mouth. Your mouth feels dry.

3  Your brain detects this and makes you feel thirsty.

On a hot day you can lose up to 3 litres of water an hour in sweat. You must drink enough water to replace it.

WATER

## Shunting blood around the body

This shows how extra blood is shunted to the muscles during exercise, using vasodilation and vasoconstriction.

blood flow

gut

muscles

**At rest**

gut

muscles

vasodilation

vasoconstriction

**During exercise**

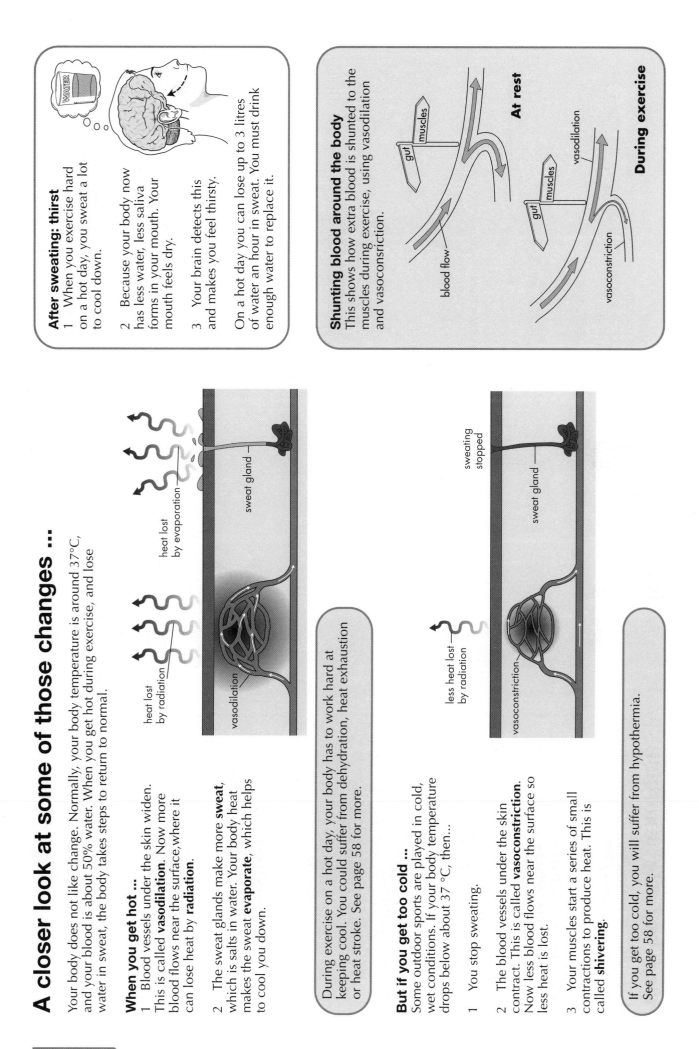

Q18, page 81

# Recovery after exercise

It takes some time for your body to recover after exercise.
These are the main changes that take place.

## Heart rate

The heart rate slows down to its normal resting rate. (You can tell by the pulse.) The fitter you are, the faster this happens.

*(Graph: Heart rate (bpm) vs Time (min). Y-axis values 60, 100, 150, 200. X-axis values 5, 10, 15, 20, 25. Labels: "less fit", "fit", "resting rates", "exercise stops")*

## Lactic acid removal

Oxygen removes lactic acid from the body. (This is called repaying the oxygen debt.) The process is faster when you do a cool down.

*(Graph: Removal of lactic acid (%) vs Time (hours). Y-axis 50, 100. X-axis 1, 2. Labels: "active recovery (cool down)", "resting recovery")*

## Muscle repair

- **Muscles** may suffer minor damage during training. Your body has to repair this. Stiffness and soreness take time to clear.

  exercise may cause microscopic tears in fibres

  stretching as part of cool down helps prevent stiffness

- The **glycogen stores** in muscles get used up during exercise. The store in the liver may also get depleted. It takes time to replace glycogen.

  A starchy snack immediately after exercise will help.

  *(Graph: Glycogen level in muscles (%) vs Time (hours). Y-axis 100. X-axis 1, 2, 3, 4. Label: "exercise stops")*

After prolonged exercise such as marathon running, it can take 48 hours for glycogen stores to recover.

## How long does recovery take?

It depends on:

- how strenuous the exercise is
- your fitness. The fitter you are the faster you recover. Allow 24 to 48 hours between training sessions for recovery, in the early stages of training.
- If you train every day, follow a heavy session one day with a light session the next.
- Even during heavy training, take one rest day a week.

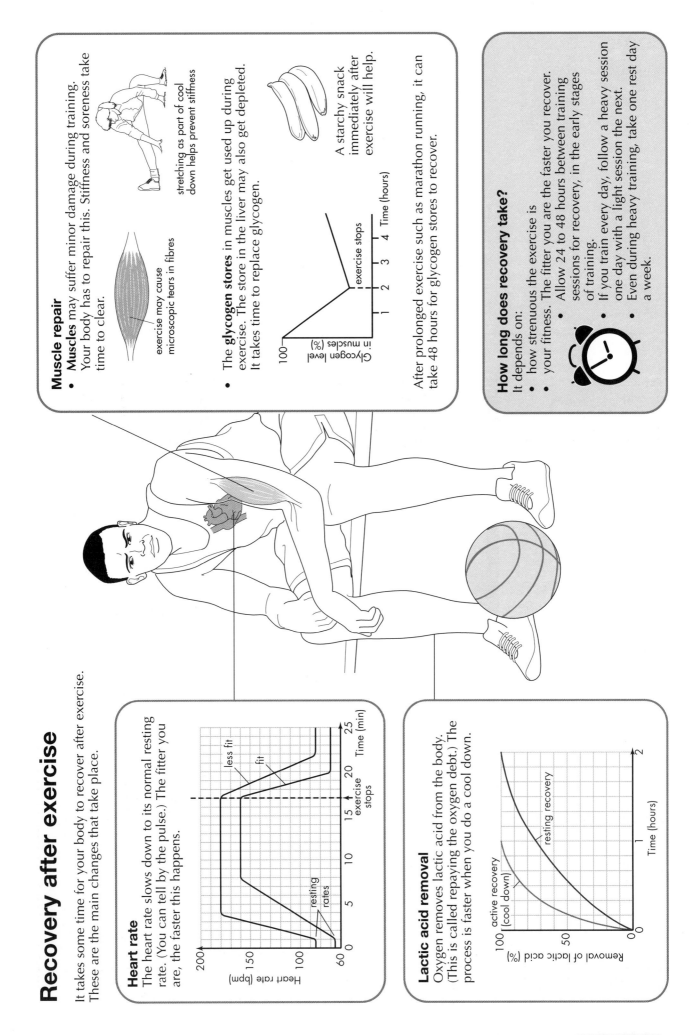

Q19, page 81

# Somatotyping

**Somatotyping** is a way to describe body build.
It looks at how fat, muscular and linear the body is, in that order.
Each is measured on a scale of 1 to 7. There are three extremes.

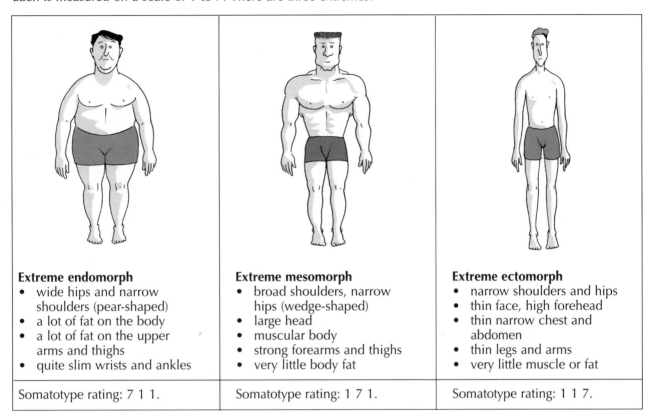

| **Extreme endomorph** | **Extreme mesomorph** | **Extreme ectomorph** |
|---|---|---|
| • wide hips and narrow shoulders (pear-shaped)<br>• a lot of fat on the body<br>• a lot of fat on the upper arms and thighs<br>• quite slim wrists and ankles | • broad shoulders, narrow hips (wedge-shaped)<br>• large head<br>• muscular body<br>• strong forearms and thighs<br>• very little body fat | • narrow shoulders and hips<br>• thin face, high forehead<br>• thin narrow chest and abdomen<br>• thin legs and arms<br>• very little muscle or fat |
| Somatotype rating: 7 1 1. | Somatotype rating: 1 7 1. | Somatotype rating: 1 1 7. |

Most people are between these extremes, with ratings such as 3 4 4 or 3 5 2.

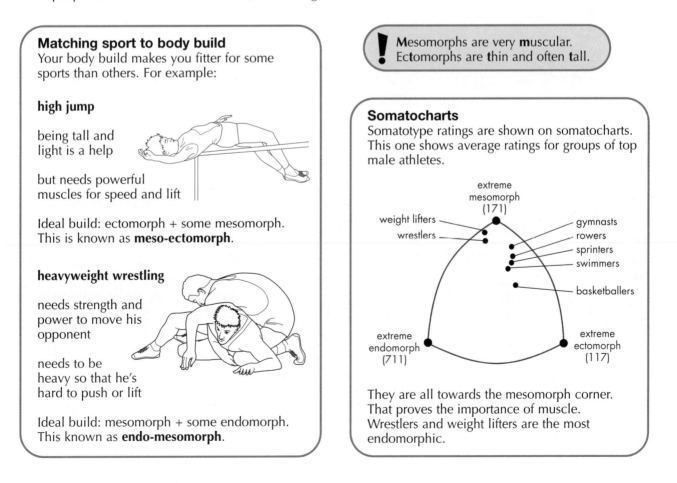

### Matching sport to body build
Your body build makes you fitter for some sports than others. For example:

**high jump**

being tall and light is a help

but needs powerful muscles for speed and lift

Ideal build: ectomorph + some mesomorph. This is known as **meso-ectomorph**.

**heavyweight wrestling**

needs strength and power to move his opponent

needs to be heavy so that he's hard to push or lift

Ideal build: mesomorph + some endomorph. This known as **endo-mesomorph**.

> **!** Mesomorphs are very **m**uscular.
> Ectomorphs are **t**hin and often **t**all.

### Somatocharts
Somatotype ratings are shown on somatocharts. This one shows average ratings for groups of top male athletes.

They are all towards the mesomorph corner. That proves the importance of muscle. Wrestlers and weight lifters are the most endomorphic.

# A closer look at fitness

## General or health-related fitness
This is the ability of your body to cope with the demands of everyday life. It has several components....

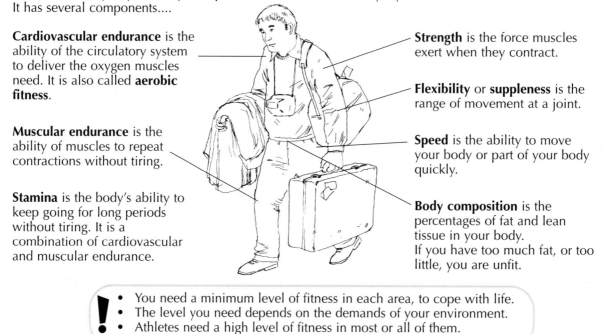

**Cardiovascular endurance** is the ability of the circulatory system to deliver the oxygen muscles need. It is also called **aerobic fitness**.

**Muscular endurance** is the ability of muscles to repeat contractions without tiring.

**Stamina** is the body's ability to keep going for long periods without tiring. It is a combination of cardiovascular and muscular endurance.

**Strength** is the force muscles exert when they contract.

**Flexibility** or **suppleness** is the range of movement at a joint.

**Speed** is the ability to move your body or part of your body quickly.

**Body composition** is the percentages of fat and lean tissue in your body. If you have too much fat, or too little, you are unfit.

! 
- You need a minimum level of fitness in each area, to cope with life.
- The level you need depends on the demands of your environment.
- Athletes need a high level of fitness in most or all of them.

## Skills-related or specific fitness
To be good at sport, you need good general fitness – see above! Skill in your sport also depends on at least some of these ...

**Explosive strength** or **power** – a combination of strength and speed.

**Agility** – the ability to change the body's position and direction fast.

**Balance** – the ability to hold a position without wobbling or falling over.

Good **co-ordination** – the ability to move body parts smoothly and accurately in response to what your senses tell you.

**Fast reactions.** Speed of reaction is the time it takes to respond to a stimulus.

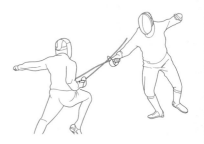

A good sense of **timing** – the ability to act at just the right moment.

Q1 and 2, page 81

# Factors affecting fitness

Being fit means being healthy too. All these factors affect fitness.

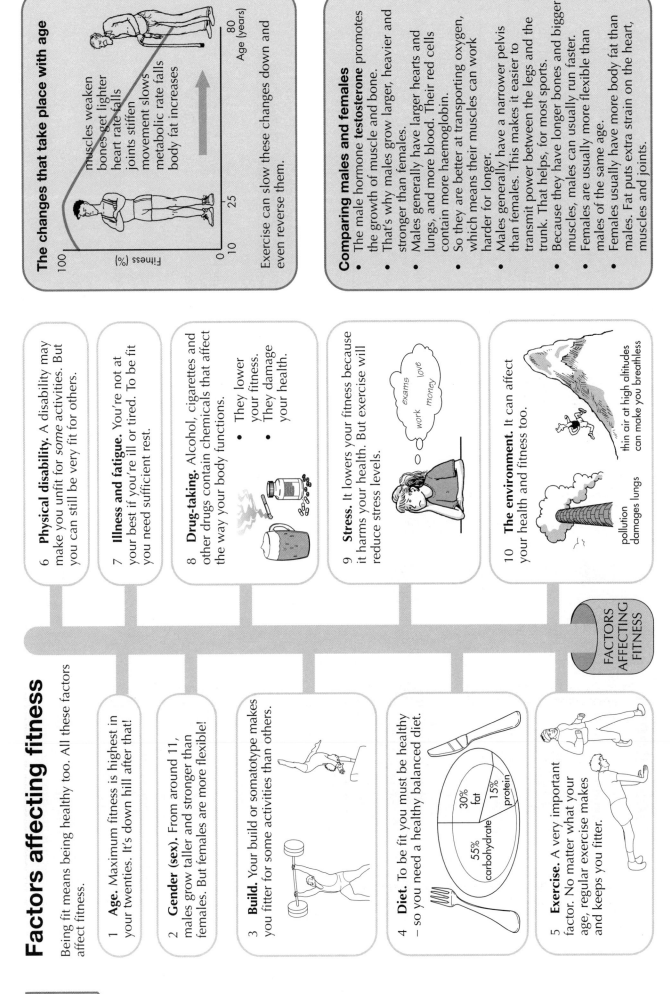

1  **Age.** Maximum fitness is highest in your twenties. It's down hill after that!

2  **Gender (sex).** From around 11, males grow taller and stronger than females. But females are more flexible!

3  **Build.** Your build or somatotype makes you fitter for some activities than others.

4  **Diet.** To be fit you must be healthy – so you need a healthy balanced diet.

55% carbohydrate
30% fat
15% protein

5  **Exercise.** A very important factor. No matter what your age, regular exercise makes and keeps you fitter.

6  **Physical disability.** A disability may make you unfit for *some* activities. But you can still be very fit for others.

7  **Illness and fatigue.** You're not at your best if you're ill or tired. To be fit you need sufficient rest.

8  **Drug-taking.** Alcohol, cigarettes and other drugs contain chemicals that affect the way your body functions.

- They lower your fitness.
- They damage your health.

9  **Stress.** It lowers your fitness because it harms your health. But exercise will reduce stress levels.

work  exams  love  money

10  **The environment.** It can affect your health and fitness too.

pollution damages lungs

thin air at high altitudes can make you breathless

FACTORS AFFECTING FITNESS

## The changes that take place with age

muscles weaken
bones get lighter
heart rate falls
joints stiffen
movement slows
metabolic rate falls
body fat increases

Fitness (%)
100
0
10  25  80
Age (years)

Exercise can slow these changes down and even reverse them.

## Comparing males and females

- The male hormone **testosterone** promotes the growth of muscle and bone.
- That's why males grow larger, heavier and stronger than females.
- Males generally have larger hearts and lungs, and more blood. Their red cells contain more haemoglobin.
- So they are better at transporting oxygen, which means their muscles can work harder for longer.
- Males generally have a narrower pelvis than females. This makes it easier to transmit power between the legs and the trunk. That helps, for most sports.
- Because they have longer bones and bigger muscles, males can usually run faster.
- Females are usually more flexible than males of the same age.
- Females usually have more body fat than males. Fat puts extra strain on the heart, muscles and joints.

Q3, page 81

# Testing aerobic fitness

**Fitness tests** help you check how fit you are, and see how your fitness improves with exercise.

The tests on this page test aerobic fitness – the fitness of your heart-lung team. The higher it is:
- the lower your heart rate will be, both resting and during exercise.
- the longer you can exercise without tiring.
- the more oxygen you use up during exercise.

### Measuring your heart rate
- It is the number of heart beats per minute.
- You can measure it at pulse points on the **carotid** and **radial** arteries.
- Press lightly on the pulse point. Count the 'beats' for 15 seconds. Multiply your count by 4. (4 × 15 seconds = 1 minute.)

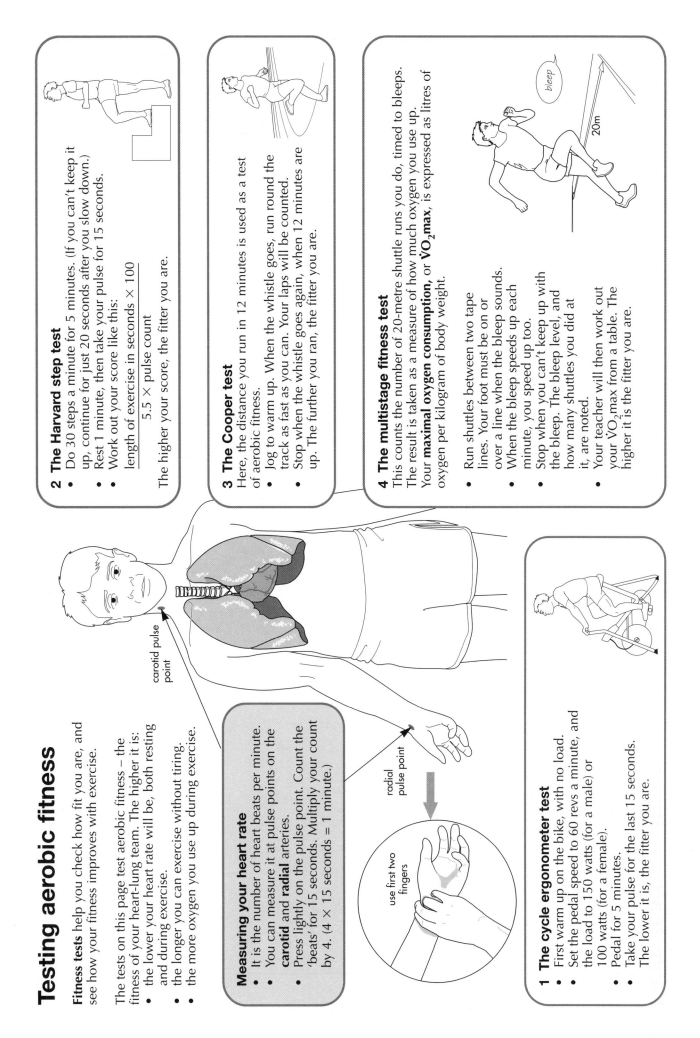

carotid pulse point

radial pulse point

use first two fingers

## 2 The Harvard step test
- Do 30 steps a minute for 5 minutes. (If you can't keep it up, continue for just 20 seconds after you slow down.)
- Rest 1 minute, then take your pulse for 15 seconds.
- Work out your score like this:

$$\frac{\text{length of exercise in seconds} \times 100}{5.5 \times \text{pulse count}}$$

The higher your score, the fitter you are.

## 3 The Cooper test
Here, the distance you run in 12 minutes is used as a test of aerobic fitness.
- Jog to warm up. When the whistle goes, run round the track as fast as you can. Your laps will be counted.
- Stop when the whistle goes again, when 12 minutes are up. The further you ran, the fitter you are.

## 4 The multistage fitness test
This counts the number of 20-metre shuttle runs you do, timed to bleeps. The result is taken as a measure of how much oxygen you use up. Your **maximal oxygen consumption**, or $\dot{V}O_2$**max**, is expressed as litres of oxygen per kilogram of body weight.

- Run shuttles between two tape lines. Your foot must be on or over a line when the bleep sounds.
- When the bleep speeds up each minute, you speed up too.
- Stop when you can't keep up with the bleep. The bleep level, and how many shuttles you did at it, are noted.
- Your teacher will then work out your $\dot{V}O_2$max from a table. The higher it is, the fitter you are.

bleep

20m

## 1 The cycle ergonometer test
- First warm up on the bike, with no load.
- Set the pedal speed to 60 revs a minute, and the load to 150 watts (for a male) or 100 watts (for a female).
- Pedal for 5 minutes.
- Take your pulse for the last 15 seconds. The lower it is, the fitter you are.

Q4, page 81

# Other tests of fitness

These 9 activities can be used as tests. But you can also do them as exercises to make you fitter!

- Tests 1–3 test the strength and/or endurance of arm and shoulder muscles.
- If the test lasts longer than 30–60 seconds it is testing endurance rather than strength.
- For each test, see how many you can do without stopping.

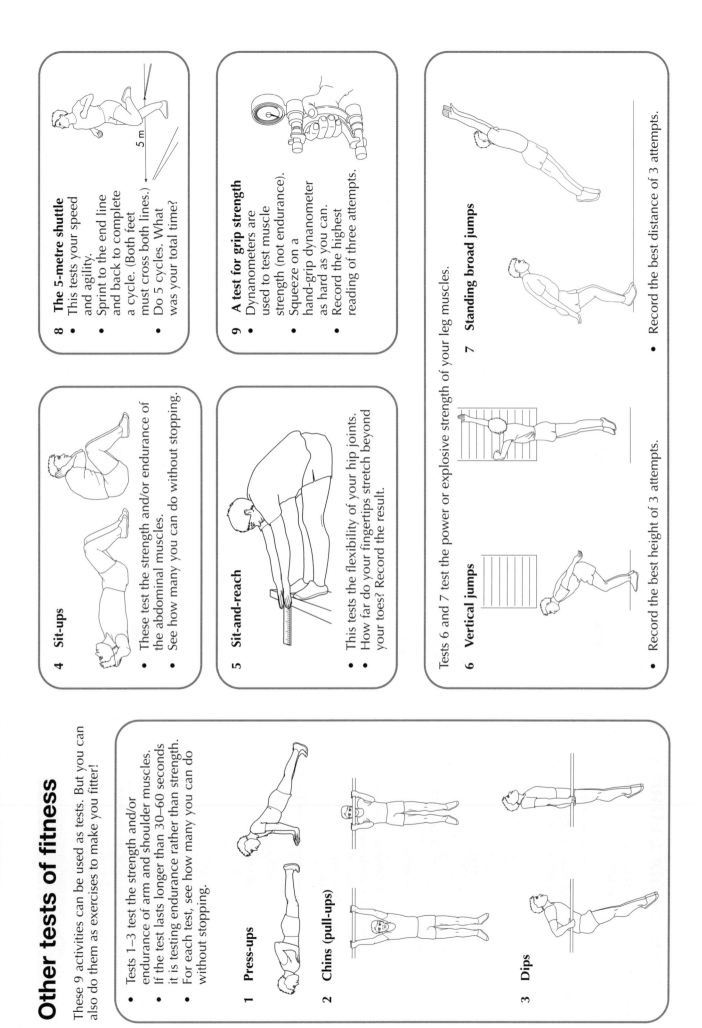

**1 Press-ups**

**2 Chins (pull-ups)**

**3 Dips**

**4 Sit-ups**

- These test the strength and/or endurance of the abdominal muscles.
- See how many you can do without stopping.

**5 Sit-and-reach**

- This tests the flexibility of your hip joints.
- How far do your fingertips stretch beyond your toes? Record the result.

Tests 6 and 7 test the power or explosive strength of your leg muscles.

**6 Vertical jumps**

- Record the best height of 3 attempts.

**7 Standing broad jumps**

- Record the best distance of 3 attempts.

**8 The 5-metre shuttle**

- This tests your speed and agility.
- Sprint to the end line and back to complete a cycle. (Both feet must cross both lines.)
- Do 5 cycles. What was your total time?

5 m

**9 A test for grip strength**

- Dynamometers are used to test muscle strength (not endurance).
- Squeeze on a hand-grip dynamometer as hard as you can.
- Record the highest reading of three attempts.

Q5, page 81

# The principles of training

**Training** is a programme of exercise to help you reach your fitness goals. It is based on four **principles**.

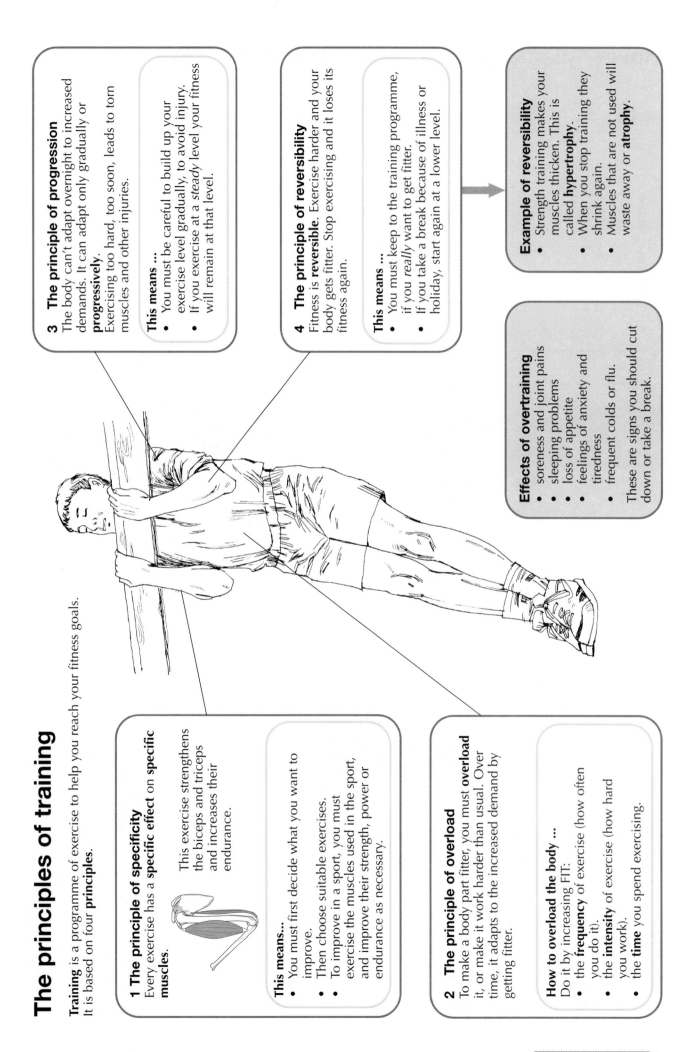

## 1 The principle of specificity

Every exercise has a **specific effect** on **specific muscles.**

This exercise strengthens the biceps and triceps and increases their endurance.

**This means...**

- You must first decide what you want to improve.
- Then choose suitable exercises.
- To improve in a sport, you must exercise the muscles used in the sport, and improve their strength, power or endurance as necessary.

## 2 The principle of overload

To make a body part fitter, you must **overload** it, or make it work harder than usual. Over time, it adapts to the increased demand by getting fitter.

**How to overload the body ...**
Do it by increasing FIT:

- the **frequency** of exercise (how often you do it).
- the **intensity** of exercise (how hard you work).
- the **time** you spend exercising.

## 3 The principle of progression

The body can't adapt overnight to increased demands. It can adapt only gradually or **progressively**.
Exercising too hard, too soon, leads to torn muscles and other injuries.

**This means ...**

- You must be careful to build up your exercise level gradually, to avoid injury.
- If you exercise at a *steady* level your fitness will remain at that level.

## 4 The principle of reversibility

Fitness is **reversible**. Exercise harder and your body gets fitter. Stop exercising and it loses its fitness again.

**This means ...**

- You must keep to the training programme, if you *really* want to get fitter.
- If you take a break because of illness or holiday, start again at a lower level.

**Example of reversibility**

- Strength training makes your muscles thicken. This is called **hypertrophy**.
- When you stop training they shrink again.
- Muscles that are not used will waste away or **atrophy**.

**Effects of overtraining**

- soreness and joint pains
- sleeping problems
- loss of appetite
- feelings of anxiety and tiredness
- frequent colds or flu.

These are signs you should cut down or take a break.

Q6 and 7, page 81

# How to plan a 6-week fitness training programme

These are the steps.

**1  Find out about the person it's for.**

This means asking questions ...

how old?

reasons for wanting to get fitter

any injuries?

play a sport?

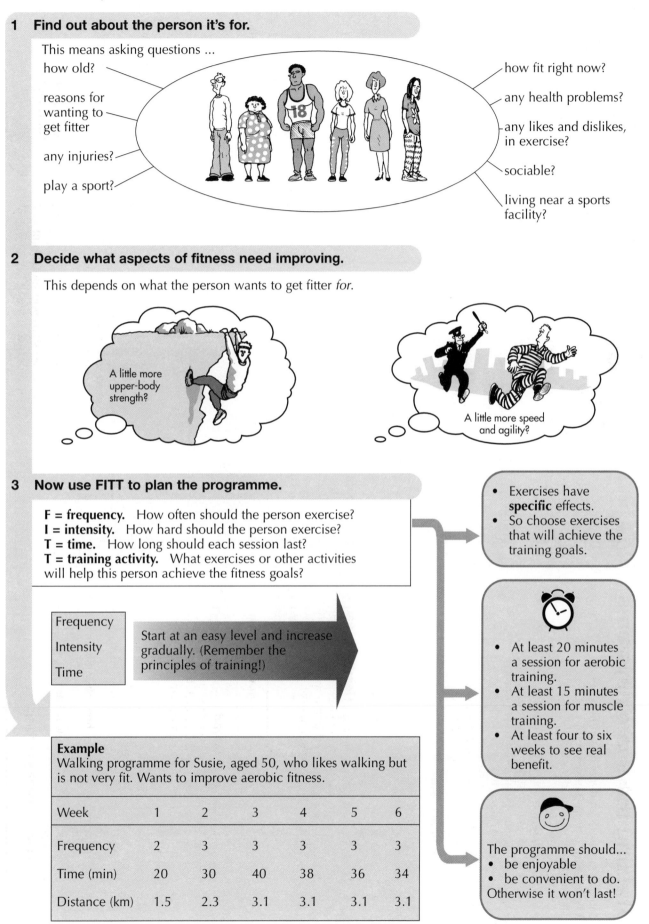

how fit right now?

any health problems?

any likes and dislikes, in exercise?

sociable?

living near a sports facility?

**2  Decide what aspects of fitness need improving.**

This depends on what the person wants to get fitter *for*.

A little more upper-body strength?

A little more speed and agility?

**3  Now use FITT to plan the programme.**

**F = frequency.**   How often should the person exercise?
**I = intensity.**   How hard should the person exercise?
**T = time.**   How long should each session last?
**T = training activity.**   What exercises or other activities will help this person achieve the fitness goals?

- Exercises have **specific** effects.
- So choose exercises that will achieve the training goals.

Frequency

Intensity

Time

Start at an easy level and increase gradually. (Remember the principles of training!)

- At least 20 minutes a session for aerobic training.
- At least 15 minutes a session for muscle training.
- At least four to six weeks to see real benefit.

**Example**
Walking programme for Susie, aged 50, who likes walking but is not very fit. Wants to improve aerobic fitness.

| Week | 1 | 2 | 3 | 4 | 5 | 6 |
|---|---|---|---|---|---|---|
| Frequency | 2 | 3 | 3 | 3 | 3 | 3 |
| Time (min) | 20 | 30 | 40 | 38 | 36 | 34 |
| Distance (km) | 1.5 | 2.3 | 3.1 | 3.1 | 3.1 | 3.1 |

The programme should...
- be enjoyable
- be convenient to do.
Otherwise it won't last!

Q8, page 81

# Training the energy systems

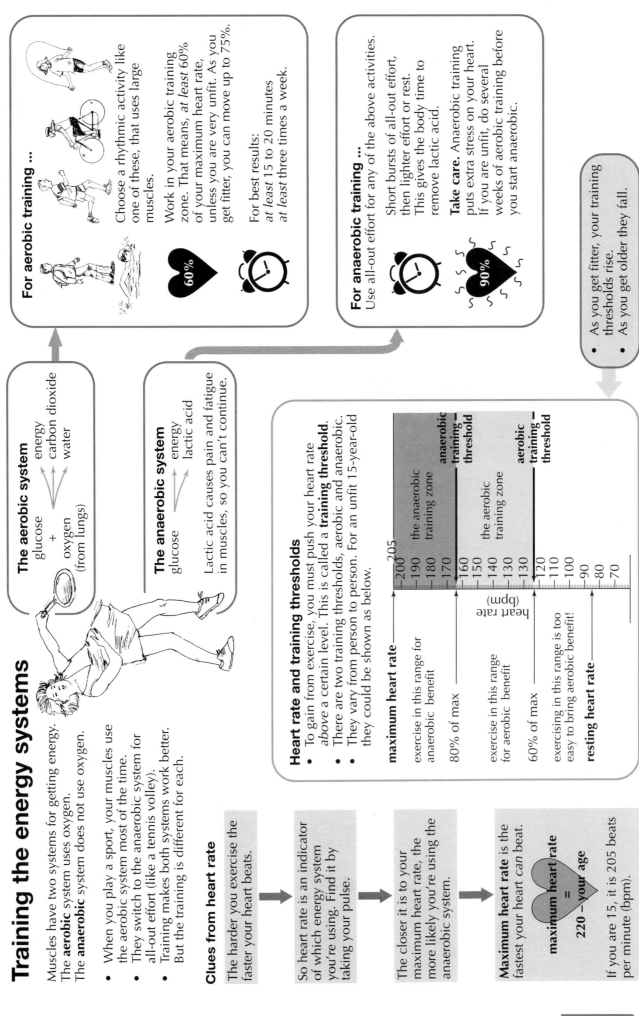

Muscles have two systems for getting energy.
The **aerobic** system uses oxygen.
The **anaerobic** system does not use oxygen.

- When you play a sport, your muscles use the aerobic system most of the time.
- They switch to the anaerobic system for all-out effort (like a tennis volley).
- Training makes both systems work better. But the training is different for each.

### The aerobic system

glucose
+
oxygen
(from lungs)

→ energy
carbon dioxide
water

### The anaerobic system

glucose → energy
lactic acid

Lactic acid causes pain and fatigue in muscles, so you can't continue.

## For aerobic training ...

Choose a rhythmic activity like one of these, that uses large muscles.

Work in your aerobic training zone. That means, *at least 60%* of your maximum heart rate, unless you are very unfit. As you get fitter, you can move up to 75%.

For best results:
*at least* 15 to 20 minutes
*at least* three times a week.

**60%**

## For anaerobic training ...

Use all-out effort for any of the above activities.

Short bursts of all-out effort, then lighter effort or rest. This gives the body time to remove lactic acid.

**Take care.** Anaerobic training puts extra stress on your heart. If you are unfit, do several weeks of aerobic training before you start anaerobic.

**90%**

- As you get fitter, your training thresholds rise.
- As you get older they fall.

## Clues from heart rate

The harder you exercise the faster your heart beats.

So heart rate is an indicator of which energy system you're using. Find it by taking your pulse.

The closer it is to your maximum heart rate, the more likely you're using the anaerobic system.

**Maximum heart rate** is the fastest your heart *can* beat.

**maximum heart rate**
**=**
**220 – your age**

If you are 15, it is 205 beats per minute (bpm).

## Heart rate and training thresholds

- To gain from exercise, you must push your heart rate *above* a certain level. This is called a **training threshold**.
- There are two training thresholds, aerobic and anaerobic.
- They vary from person to person. For an unfit 15-year-old they could be shown as below.

**maximum heart rate** ——— 205

the anaerobic training zone

**anaerobic training threshold**

exercise in this range for anaerobic benefit

80% of max

the aerobic training zone

**aerobic training threshold**

exercise in this range for aerobic benefit

60% of max

exercising in this range is too easy to bring aerobic benefit!

**resting heart rate**

heart rate (bpm)

200 190 180 170 160 150 140 130 120 110 100 90 80 70

Q9, page 82

# Four methods of energy training

This page shows four methods of training the energy systems.
- **Continuous training** and **aerobics** are for the aerobic system.
- **Fartlek training** and **interval training** can be used for both systems, depending on the speed you work at.

## 1 Continuous training
- You walk, jog, cycle or swim at a *steady* pace, without rest.
- To overload, increase the time, distance, speed or frequency.

**Advantages** ✓
- Great for aerobic fitness.
- No need for special equipment.
- Good for burning off body fat.

**Disadvantages** ✗
- Can be boring.
- Does not improve sprint speed, which is needed for many sports.

## 2 Aerobics
- You exercise every part of the body.
- You usually work in a class in time to music.

**Advantages** ✓
- Good fun.
- Classes can be sociable.
- Appeals to lots of women.

**Disadvantages** ✗
- Jumping and stamping can jar bones and damage joints.
- The class may be a mixture of fitness levels. Some people may get left behind.

For safety, work on a sprung hardwood floor or soft mat. Or choose **low impact** aerobics.

## 3 Fartlek training
- This is based on changes of speed.
- You can use it for things like running, cycling and skiing.
- Overload by increasing times, speeds, or the difficulty of the terrain. For example run uphill or through sand.

**Example:** Part of a 30-minute Fartlek running session

| 5 min gentle jog | 5 min fast walk | 5 min fast jog with 50 m sprints every 200 m | 5 min uphill jog with 10 fast strides every minute | and so on ... |

**Advantages** ✓
- Good training for sports with many changes of speed.
- You can change the mix of fast and bits, slow work to suit a sport.
- The changes of pace make it interesting.

**Disadvantages** ✗
- Coaches can't really tell how hard an athlete is working.
- It's easy to skip the tough so you need determination.

## 4 Interval training
- This has a fixed pattern of fast and slow work.
- You can use it for things like running and swimming.
- Each repetition of the pattern is called a **rep**. You must complete a **set** of reps before you can take a rest.
- Overload by doing more reps or sets or both, or by spending less time on slow work and resting.

**Example:** interval training to improve acceleration at the start of a sprint race

| 30 metre sprint | then ... | 30 seconds easy jogging |

This is one **rep**.
Repeat 10 times to make a **set**.
Then take a 2-minute **rest**.
Do 3 sets altogether.

**Advantages** ✓
- You can mix anaerobic and aerobic work.
- It is easy to see when an athlete is giving up.

**Disadvantage** ✗
- It's hard to keep going. You need determination!

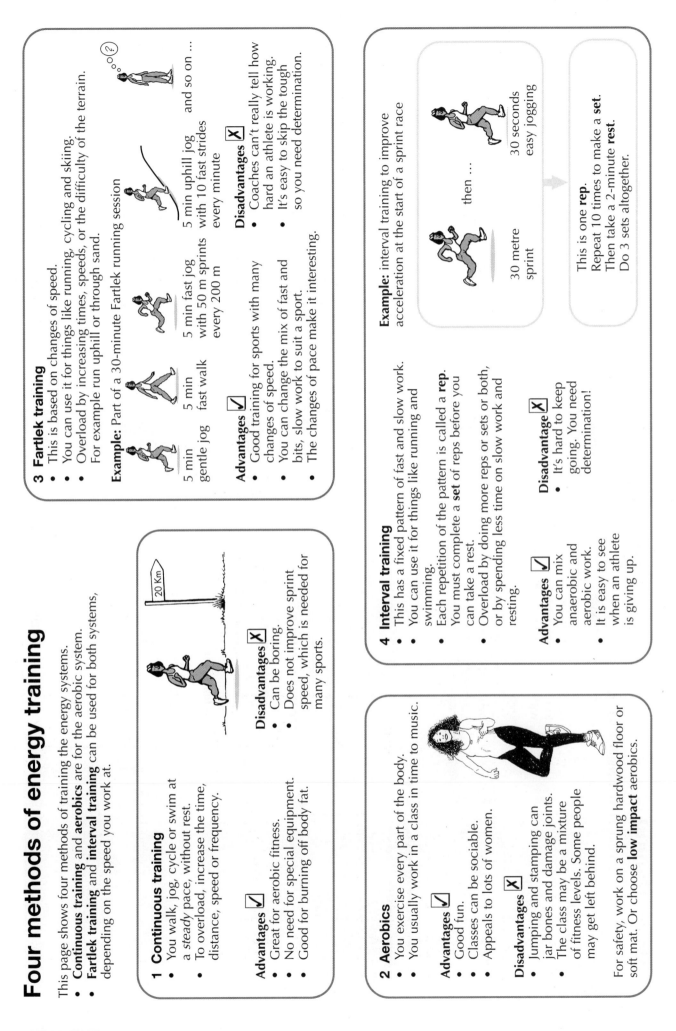

Q10, page 82

# Muscle training

For most sports your muscles need **strength** and **endurance**.

**endurance**
the ability of muscles to repeat a contraction without getting tired

**strength**
the ability to contract with force. There are three kinds of strength.

**dynamic strength**
the strength you need to move a heavy load.

**explosive strength** or **power**
the strength you need for a single explosive act, such as a discus throw or shot putt.

**static strength**
the strength you need to push or pull a heavy object, or hold up a heavy weight.

**Improving muscle fitness**
- You can do exercises to improve both strength and endurance.
- The exercises all involve pushing or pulling or lifting a **load**. This can be...

your body weight    free weights    machine weights

**weight training**

**To improve endurance**
Use a load that's light enough to allow many repetitions.

All these exercises improve endurance. Most improve strength up to a point.

**To improve strength**
Use a heavier load and a small number of repetitions.
- Hold a heavy load stationary to improve static strength.
- Move it to improve dynamic strength.
- Move it very fast to improve power.

For muscle training sessions, build up to...
*at least* 15 min a session.
*at least* 3 sessions a week.

**Using your body weight**

**Advantages** ☑
- Easy to do anywhere.
- You can use it to increase both strength and endurance.
- You can increase the strength aspect by strapping on weights, or asking a partner to press down on your body.

**Disadvantage** ☒
- You need determination to keep going!

**Weight training**

**Advantages** ☑
- It's easy to tell what load you are using.
- It's easy to increase the load.
- It's easy to work on different muscle groups, to suit a sport.

**Disadvantages** ☒
- You can injure yourself badly by using too heavy a load. *Not suitable* for people under 16. Your frame is still immature. You can get injured too easily.

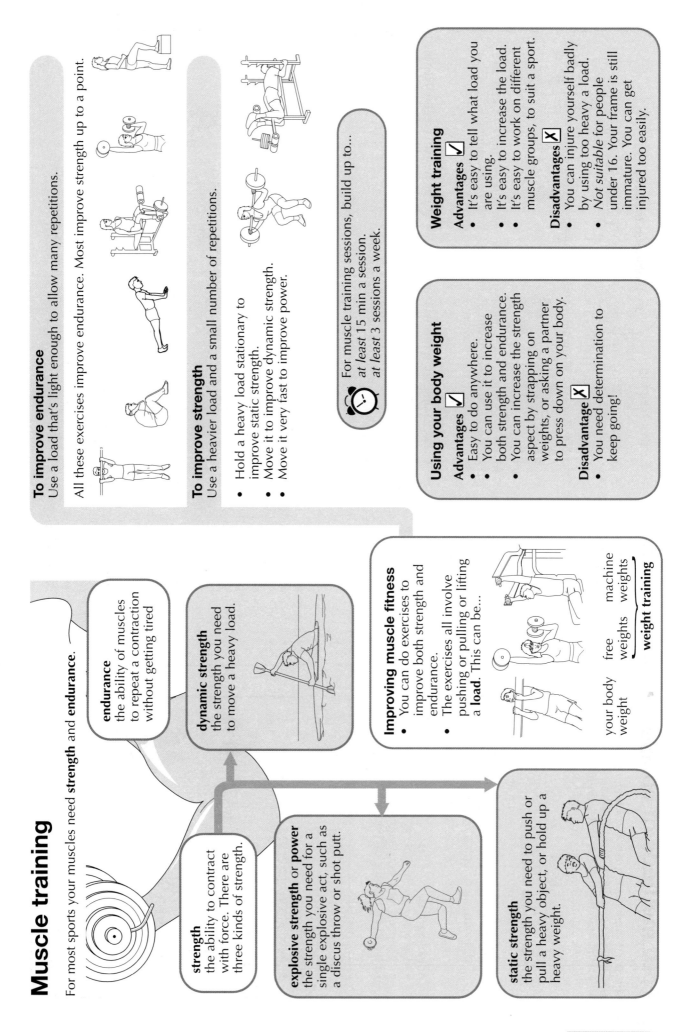

Q11, page 82 ▷

# A closer look at muscle training exercises

All muscle training falls into three types, depending on the muscle contraction.

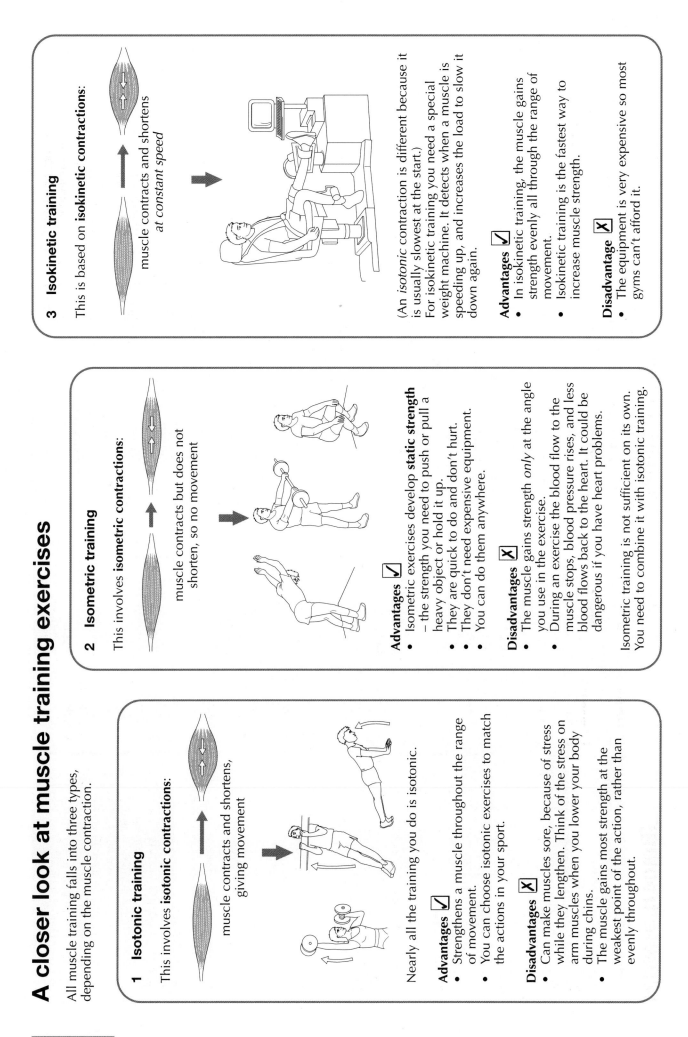

## 1 Isotonic training

This involves **isotonic contractions**:

muscle contracts and shortens, giving movement

Nearly all the training you do is isotonic.

**Advantages** ✓
- Strengthens a muscle throughout the range of movement.
- You can choose isotonic exercises to match the actions in your sport.

**Disadvantages** ✗
- Can make muscles sore, because of stress while they lengthen. Think of the stress on arm muscles when you lower your body during chins.
- The muscle gains most strength at the weakest point of the action, rather than evenly throughout.

## 2 Isometric training

This involves **isometric contractions**:

muscle contracts but does not shorten, so no movement

**Advantages** ✓
- Isometric exercises develop **static strength** – the strength you need to push or pull a heavy object or hold it up.
- They are quick to do and don't hurt.
- They don't need expensive equipment.
- You can do them anywhere.

**Disadvantages** ✗
- The muscle gains strength *only* at the angle you use in the exercise.
- During an exercise the blood flow to the muscle stops, blood pressure rises, and less blood flows back to the heart. It could be dangerous if you have heart problems.

Isometric training is not sufficient on its own. You need to combine it with isotonic training.

## 3 Isokinetic training

This is based on **isokinetic contractions**:

muscle contracts and shortens *at constant speed*

(An *isotonic* contraction is different because it is usually slowest at the start.) For isokinetic training you need a special weight machine. It detects when a muscle is speeding up, and increases the load to slow it down again.

**Advantages** ✓
- In isokinetic training, the muscle gains strength evenly all through the range of movement.
- Isokinetic training is the fastest way to increase muscle strength.

**Disadvantage** ✗
- The equipment is very expensive so most gyms can't afford it.

Q12, page 82

# Circuit training

**Circuit training** is one way to organise muscle training.
- A circuit usually has 8 to 15 **stations**, arranged in a loop.
- You do different exercises at each station.

The circuit below is designed to improve muscular endurance, and, to some extent, aerobic fitness and muscular strength.

① press-ups

② vertical jump

③ sit-ups

④ dorsal raises

⑤ ski-jumps

⑥ chins

⑦ shuttle

⑧ step-ups

### Ways to do the circuit
- Do a given number of reps (repetitions) at each station.
- Or spend 1 minute at each station, and do as many reps as you can.
- You can include a short rest between stations.

### Ways to overload
- Do more reps at each station.
- Complete the circuit in less time.
- Reduce the rest time between stations.
- Repeat the circuit.

### Designing a circuit
- Decide what type of fitness you want to improve.
- Choose exercises that will do this.
- Include exercises for opposing muscle groups. For example hamstrings *and* quadriceps.
- Exercise a different muscle group at each station, to reduce fatigue.
- Don't forget a warm up and cool down.

### Circuits for sports
You can also design a circuit to suit a sport.
- Include exercises for all the muscle groups used in the sport, and shuttle runs for speed.
- Use some stations for skills practice. For example passing, dribbling and heading for football.

### Advantages ✓
- Circuit training can include a big variety of exercises, which makes it fun.
- It is very adaptable. You can design a circuit to develop one or more aspects of fitness, or to suit a sport.
- It is an efficient way to use training time.
- The circuit can be indoors or outdoors. You could create an effective circuit in your living room!
- You can include weights and exercise bikes.

### Disadvantages ✗
- It can take a lot of time and effort to set up a circuit.
- Good planning is needed to stop people getting in each other's way.

# Improving flexibility

**Flexibility** is the range of movement at a joint. Good flexibility helps in most sports.

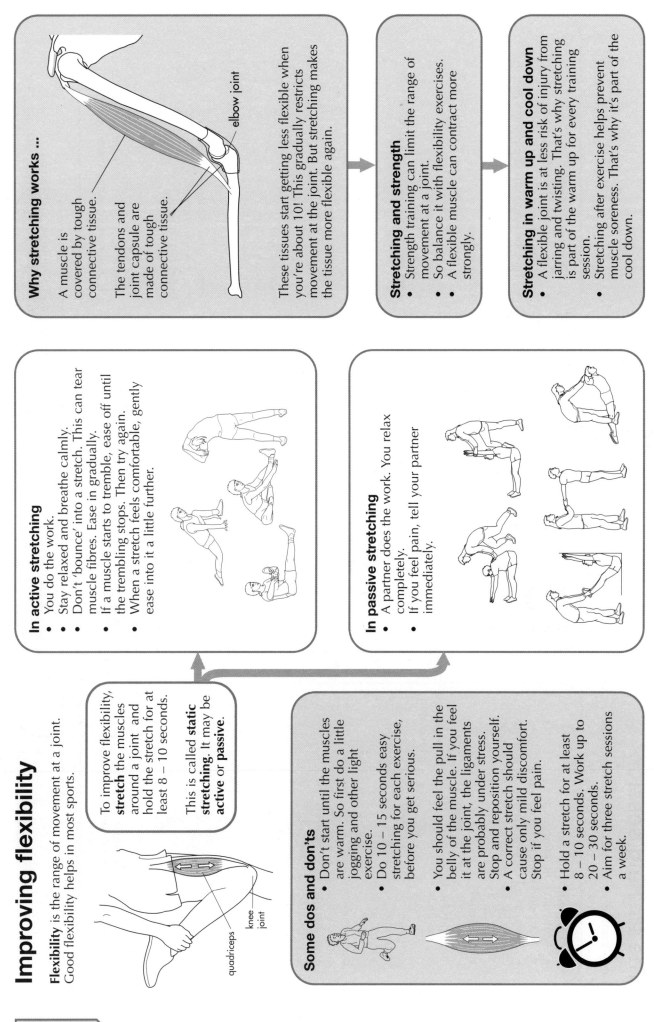

quadriceps

knee joint

To improve flexibility, **stretch** the muscles around a joint and hold the stretch for at least 8 – 10 seconds.

This is called **static stretching**. It may be **active** or **passive**.

## Why stretching works ...

A muscle is covered by tough connective tissue.

The tendons and joint capsule are made of tough connective tissue.

elbow joint

These tissues start getting less flexible when you're about 10! This gradually restricts movement at the joint. But stretching makes the tissue more flexible again.

## Stretching and strength

- Strength training can limit the range of movement at a joint.
- So balance it with flexibility exercises.
- A flexible muscle can contract more strongly.

## Stretching in warm up and cool down

- A flexible joint is at less risk of injury from jarring and twisting. That's why stretching is part of the warm up for every training session.
- Stretching after exercise helps prevent muscle soreness. That's why it's part of the cool down.

## In active stretching

- You do the work.
- Stay relaxed and breathe calmly.
- Don't 'bounce' into a stretch. This can tear muscle fibres. Ease in gradually.
- If a muscle starts to tremble, ease off until the trembling stops. Then try again.
- When a stretch feels comfortable, gently ease into it a little further.

## In passive stretching

- A partner does the work. You relax completely.
- If you feel pain, tell your partner immediately.

## Some dos and don'ts

- Don't start until the muscles are warm. So first do a little jogging and other light exercise.
- Do 10 – 15 seconds easy stretching for each exercise, before you get serious.
- You should feel the pull in the belly of the muscle. If you feel it at the joint, the ligaments are probably under stress. Stop and reposition yourself.
- A correct stretch should cause only mild discomfort. Stop if you feel pain.
- Hold a stretch for at least 8 – 10 seconds. Work up to 20 – 30 seconds.
- Aim for three stretch sessions a week.

Q14, page 82

# The training session

Every training session should have three parts.

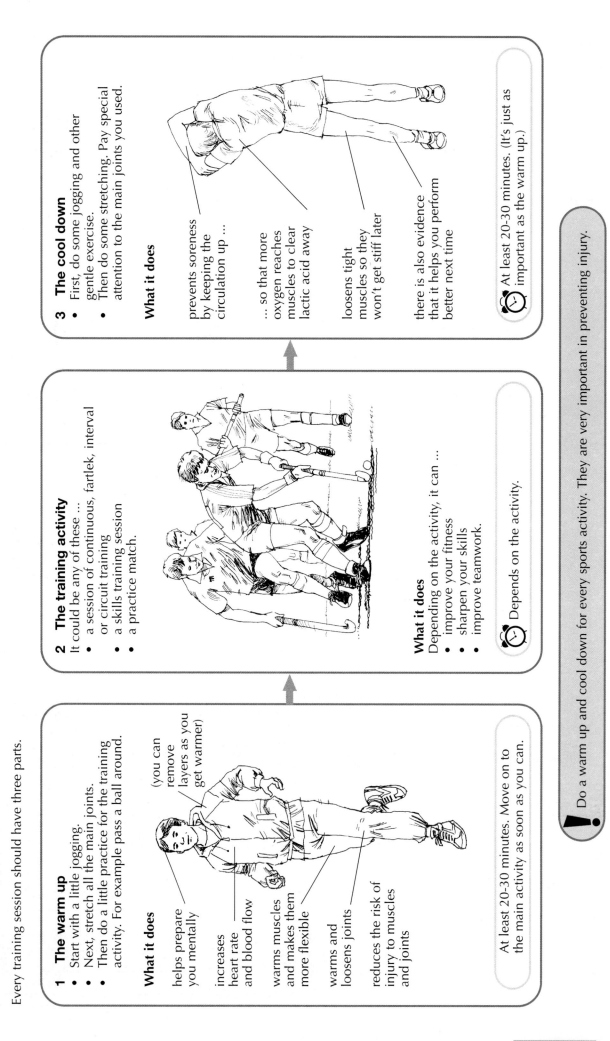

## 1 The warm up
- Start with a little jogging.
- Next, stretch all the main joints.
- Then do a little practice for the training activity. For example pass a ball around.

**What it does**

helps prepare you mentally

increases heart rate and blood flow

warms muscles and makes them more flexible

warms and loosens joints

reduces the risk of injury to muscles and joints

(you can remove layers as you get warmer)

At least 20-30 minutes. Move on to the main activity as soon as you can.

## 2 The training activity
It could be any of these ...
- a session of continuous, fartlek, interval or circuit training
- a skills training session
- a practice match.

**What it does**

Depending on the activity, it can ...
- improve your fitness
- sharpen your skills
- improve teamwork.

Depends on the activity.

## 3 The cool down
- First, do some jogging and other gentle exercise.
- Then do some stretching. Pay special attention to the main joints you used.

**What it does**

prevents soreness by keeping the circulation up ...

... so that more oxygen reaches muscles to clear lactic acid away

loosens tight muscles so they won't get stiff later

there is also evidence that it helps you perform better next time

At least 20-30 minutes. (It's just as important as the warm up.)

Do a warm up and cool down for every sports activity. They are very important in preventing injury.

Q15, page 82

# Seasonal training

- Many sports are **seasonal**. Netball and rugby are played in winter, cricket in summer.
- For the players, the year is divided into stages.
- The length of each stage may vary from sport to sport.

**The player's year**

Preparation
- out-of-season (6 weeks)
- pre-season (6 weeks)

Competition (32 weeks)

Recuperation (8 weeks)

**Note**
*All* athletes divide their year into stages like these, based around the main events they want to enter.

**Out-of-season preparation**
Aim: a high level of general fitness, through ...

25Km

mainly carbohydrate

continuous training for aerobic fitness

strength training for major muscle groups

a healthy diet

**Pre-season preparation**
Aim: peak fitness for the sport, through ...

anaerobic training (short fast sprints)

extra strength and power training for key muscles

skills training, with training circuits and practice matches

**Competition**
Aim: to win! Through ...

playing a couple of matches a week

training to maintain fitness

care to avoid injury and fatigue

**Recuperation**
Aim: complete recovery from competition, through:

rest, relaxation, and other sports to maintain a level of fitness

With care, the athlete can be in peak condition for the main events of the season.

100

performance level (%)

preparation    competition

Players and athletes may have to travel abroad to train and compete. This means ...
- extra expense
- time needed to acclimatise to a new environment.

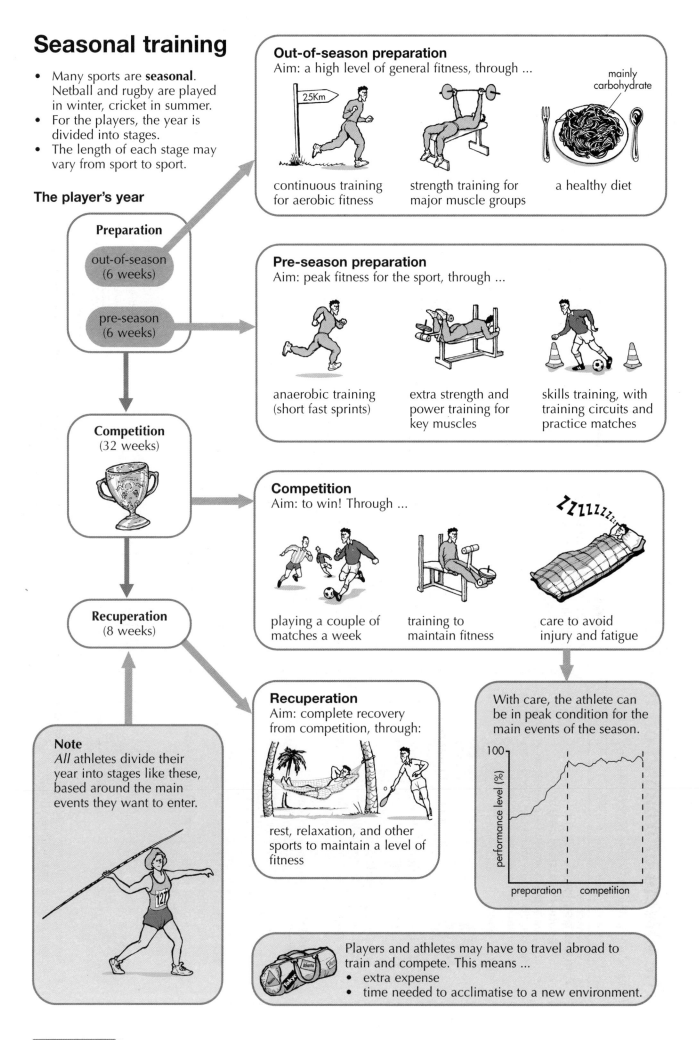

Q16, page 82

# The effects of training on the body

Months of training can cause big changes in the body.

## Aerobic training

### ... and the circulatory system

- The heart grows larger. Its walls grow a little thicker. So it can hold more blood and contract more strongly. It's now a better pump.

the heart

before training — after training

- The body makes more blood, with more red cells in it. So more oxygen can be carried.
- Arteries grow larger and more elastic. So blood pressure falls.
- The resting heart rate falls.
- The heart rate returns to normal more quickly, after exercise.

### ... and the respiratory system

- The rib muscles and diaphragm grow stronger. So the chest cavity gets larger when you breathe in.
- This means the lungs can expand further. Vital capacity increases. More oxygen can be taken in with each breath and more carbon dioxide removed.
- More capillaries grow around the alveoli. This means more blood is available for gas exchange.

capillaries around the alveoli

before training — after training

- Because gas exchange is speeded up, you can exercise for longer without tiring.

## Anaerobic training

- The heart walls get thicker, to cope with the strain of all-out effort.
- The muscles get better at tolerating lactic acid, and more efficient at clearing it away. So all-out effort can continue for longer.

## Endurance training for muscles

- More capillaries form around the muscles, so more blood reaches them with oxygen and food.
- The muscles get better at using fat for energy.
- They also get more efficient at using oxygen, so can work harder for longer without tiring.
- The overall result is that the body's maximal oxygen consumption ($\dot{V}O_2$max) increases.

## Strength training for muscles

- It makes muscles thicker, so they contract more strongly. The increase in size is called **hypertrophy**.
- The tendons get bigger and stronger too.

## Body fat

- Training causes body fat to burn up faster even when you're at rest.
- It burns up faster during exercise too, since muscles get better at using fat for energy. You get slimmer as a result.

## Joints

- Training makes the ligaments at joints stronger.
- It also makes the cartilage thicker, so bones are less likely to jar.
- Regular stretching increases the range of movement at a joint.

## Bones

- Training makes bones stronger. The cells that make bone work harder under stress.

Q17, page 82

# The foods your body needs

Your body needs four kinds of **nutrients** for energy, to grow, and to repair itself. It also needs **water** and **fibre**.

## The nutrients

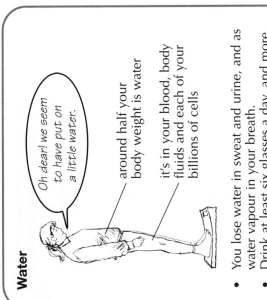

### 1 Carbohydrates
They are found in sweet and starchy foods. In your gut they break down to **glucose** which is used for energy (page 16).

### 2 Fats
Fats can also be used for energy. The fitter you are, the more readily your muscles burn up fats in place of glucose.

### 3 Proteins
Proteins are used to build and repair muscles and other tissues, and to make blood. Your body can also use them for energy, if it runs out of carbohydrates and fats.

### 4 Vitamins and minerals
Your body needs tiny amounts of vitamins and minerals.

| Substance | Where you find it ... | Why you need it ... | A shortage leads to ... |
|---|---|---|---|
| vitamin A | fish, liver, vegetables, eggs, milk | to see in dim light, and for healthy skin | night blindness, flaking skin |
| vitamin C | oranges and other citrus fruits, vegetables | for healthy skin and gums, and to help wounds heal | scurvy |
| vitamin D | made by skin in sunshine; found in milk, fish, liver, eggs | for strong bones and teeth (you can't absorb calcium without it) | rickets |
| calcium | milk, cheese, dried fish, sardines, green vegetables | for strong bones and teeth, and for muscle contractions | fragile bones |
| iron | liver, beans, lentils, green vegetables; added to bread | for the haemoglobin in red cells | tiredness and anaemia |
| iodine | sea food, vegetables grown near the sea | for hormones that control the rate at which you burn food for energy | a swollen thyroid gland (goitre) |

## Water

*Oh dear! we seem to have put on a little water.*

around half your body weight is water

it's in your blood, body fluids and each of your billions of cells

- You lose water in sweat and urine, and as water vapour in your breath.
- Drink at least six glasses a day, and more when you exercise.

## Fibre

Fibre is **cellulose** from the cell walls of plants. You can't digest it, but...
- it clears out your gut, which prevents constipation and bowel cancer
- it makes you feel full, so you eat less, and that keeps you slim.

Q18, page 82

# A balanced diet

Healthy eating means a balanced diet, which

- has the right mix of nutrients, fibre and water
- matches your energy needs.

## The right mix

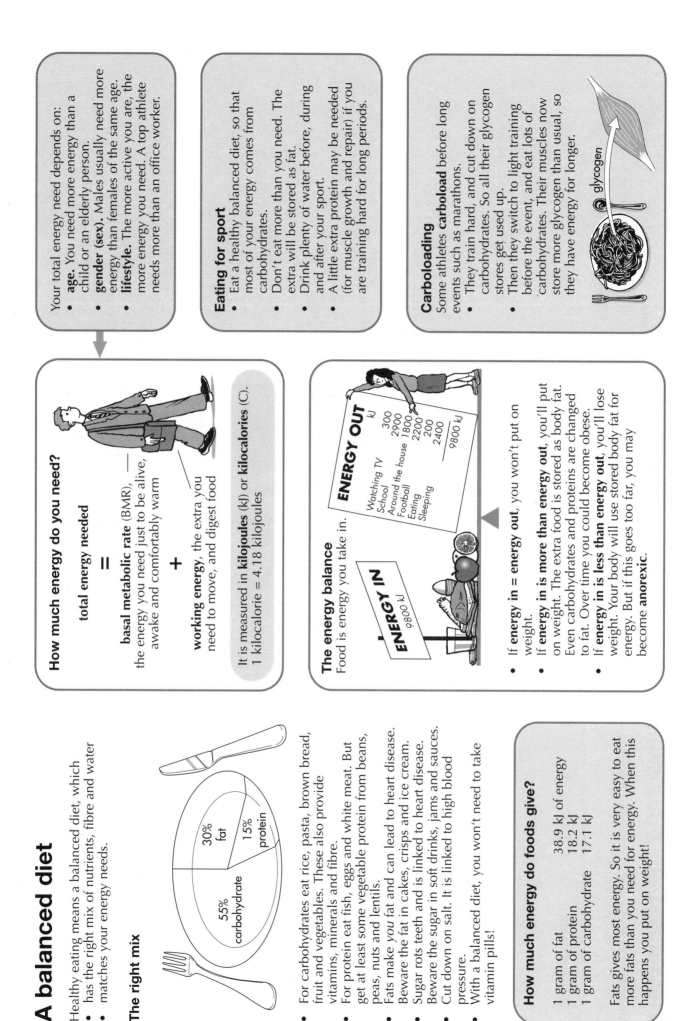

55% carbohydrate

30% fat

15% protein

- For carbohydrates eat rice, pasta, brown bread, fruit and vegetables. These also provide vitamins, minerals and fibre.
- For protein eat fish, eggs and white meat. But get at least some vegetable protein from beans, peas, nuts and lentils.
- Fats make *you* fat and can lead to heart disease. Beware the fat in cakes, crisps and ice cream.
- Sugar rots teeth and is linked to heart disease.
- Beware the sugar in soft drinks, jams and sauces.
- Cut down on salt. It is linked to high blood pressure.
- With a balanced diet, you won't need to take vitamin pills!

## How much energy do foods give?

1 gram of fat          38.9 kJ of energy
1 gram of protein      18.2 kJ
1 gram of carbohydrate 17.1 kJ

Fats gives most energy. So it is very easy to eat more fats than you need for energy. When this happens you put on weight!

## How much energy do you need?

total energy needed

=

**basal metabolic rate** (BMR), — the energy you need just to be alive, awake and comfortably warm

+

**working energy**, the extra you need to move, and digest food

It is measured in **kilojoules** (kJ) or **kilocalories** (C). 1 kilocalorie = 4.18 kilojoules

## The energy balance

Food is energy you take in.

**ENERGY IN**
9800 kJ

**ENERGY OUT**
kJ

| | |
|---|---|
| Watching TV | 300 |
| School | 2900 |
| Around the house | 1800 |
| Football | 2200 |
| Eating | 200 |
| Sleeping | 2400 |
| | 9800 kJ |

- If **energy in = energy out**, you won't put on weight.
- If **energy in is more than energy out**, you'll put on weight. The extra food is stored as body fat. Even carbohydrates and proteins are changed to fat. Over time you could become obese.
- If **energy in is less than energy out**, you'll lose weight. Your body will use stored body fat for energy. But if this goes too far, you may become **anorexic**.

Your total energy need depends on:

- **age.** You need more energy than a child or an elderly person.
- **gender (sex).** Males usually need more energy than females of the same age.
- **lifestyle.** The more active you are, the more energy you need. A top athlete needs more than an office worker.

## Eating for sport

- Eat a healthy balanced diet, so that most of your energy comes from carbohydrates.
- Don't eat more than you need. The extra will be stored as fat.
- Drink plenty of water before, during and after your sport.
- A little extra protein may be needed (for muscle growth and repair) if you are training hard for long periods.

## Carboloading

Some athletes **carboload** before long events such as marathons.

- They train hard, and cut down on carbohydrates. Their muscles now store more glycogen than usual, so they have energy for longer.
- Then they switch to light training before the event, and eat lots of carbohydrates. So all their glycogen stores get used up.

glycogen

Q19, page 82

# Weight and weight control

Your weight depends on several factors:

**height** and **frame size**. The longer and thicker your bones the more you'll weigh.

**gender (sex)**. Males are usually heavier than females of the same height.

how much **fat** you have.

**muscle girth**. The larger it is, the heavier your muscles are. (Muscles are heavier than fat.)

## Your optimum weight

- Weight charts show what weight you *should* be, for your height and build. You can find these charts in the doctor's surgery.
- If you weigh more, you are **overweight**. If less, you are **underweight**.
- If you are overweight, the extra weight puts a strain on your heart, muscles, bones and joints. Exercise becomes more difficult.
- If you are underweight, your muscles are probably small and weak. Exercise will leave you weak and tired.
- This means your weight has a big effect on your performance in sport.
- To some extent, your weight depends on your parents. You inherit your build from them.
- But you can also control your weight through exercise and healthy eating.

## Body composition and fitness

- You could be just the right *weight*, but unfit because you have lots of fat and small weak muscles.
- So **body composition** gives a better idea of fitness. It states what percentage of your body weight is fat.
- A skinfold test is used to estimate it.

| The result | % fat for a male | for a female |
|---|---|---|
| okay | 13 – 15 % | 18 – 20% |
| overfat | over 15% | over 20% |
| obese | over 20% | over 30% |

Using calipers for the skinfold test

## Obesity

**Obesity** is a severe overweight condition of the body.

- It is usually caused by eating too much.
- It puts a strain on the heart, muscles, bones and ligaments.
- Exercise gets difficult or even dangerous.
- Obesity can lead to joint and back injuries, heart attacks, strokes and other problems.

## Anorexia

- Anorexia means you have far too little fat.
- It's caused by harsh dieting.
- Without food, your body starts to use up stored fat for energy.
- When this runs out it will use proteins from body tissues. Organs stop working. You die.
- Anorexia leaves you weak and tired, with a weak immune system.

## How exercise affects your weight

- Regular exercise increases your **basal metabolic rate**. You burn up stored fat faster even when you're resting.
- It also reduces the appetite.
- Your muscles grow with exercise. They weigh more than fat but take up less space. So you won't lose much weight at the start but you'll look slimmer.

## How to lose weight

55% carbohydrate
30% fat
15% protein

a **healthy balanced diet** + **regular exercise**
(a little less than usual)        (more than usual!)

Q20, page 82

# Skill in sport

The word **skill** is used in three different ways in sport.

**1  Skill is the learned ability to bring about the result you want, with maximum certainty and efficiency.**

For example skill in tennis is something you learn. You weren't born with it.

For each shot you have an aim in mind, and you are likely to achieve it.

You perform the actions efficiently, without wasting any energy.

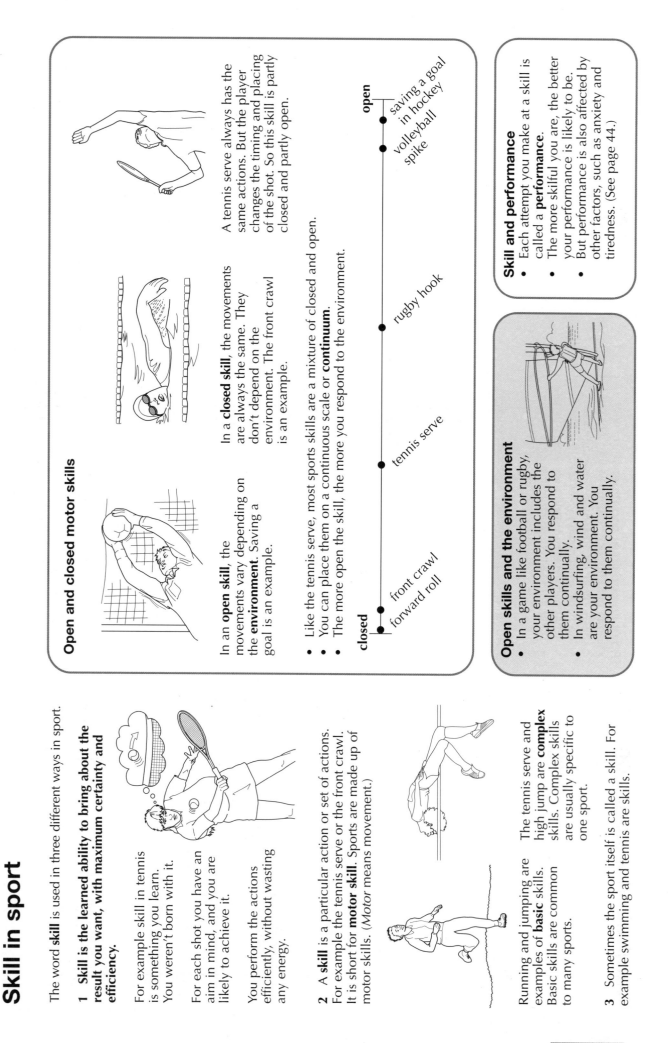

**2**  A **skill** is a particular action or set of actions. For example the tennis serve or the front crawl. It is short for **motor skill**. Sports are made up of motor skills. (*Motor* means movement.)

Running and jumping are examples of **basic** skills. Basic skills are common to many sports.

The tennis serve and high jump are **complex** skills. Complex skills are usually specific to one sport.

**3**  Sometimes the sport itself is called a skill. For example swimming and tennis are skills.

## Open and closed motor skills

In an **open skill**, the movements vary depending on the **environment**. Saving a goal is an example.

In a **closed skill**, the movements are always the same. They don't depend on the environment. The front crawl is an example.

A tennis serve always has the same actions. But the player changes the timing and placing of the shot. So this skill is partly closed and partly open.

- Like the tennis serve, most sports skills are a mixture of closed and open.
- You can place them on a continuous scale or **continuum**.
- The more open the skill, the more you respond to the environment.

**open**
- saving a goal in hockey
- volleyball spike

- rugby hook

- tennis serve

**closed**
- front crawl
- forward roll

## Open skills and the environment

- In a game like football or rugby, your environment includes the other players. You respond to them continually.
- In windsurfing, wind and water are your environment. You respond to them continually.

## Skill and performance

- Each attempt you make at a skill is called a **performance**.
- The more skilful you are, the better your performance is likely to be.
- But performance is also affected by other factors, such as anxiety and tiredness. (See page 44.)

Q1, page 83

# Information processing

When you are learning and playing a sport, you use your **information processing system**. This system has four parts. Your brain is in control of it.

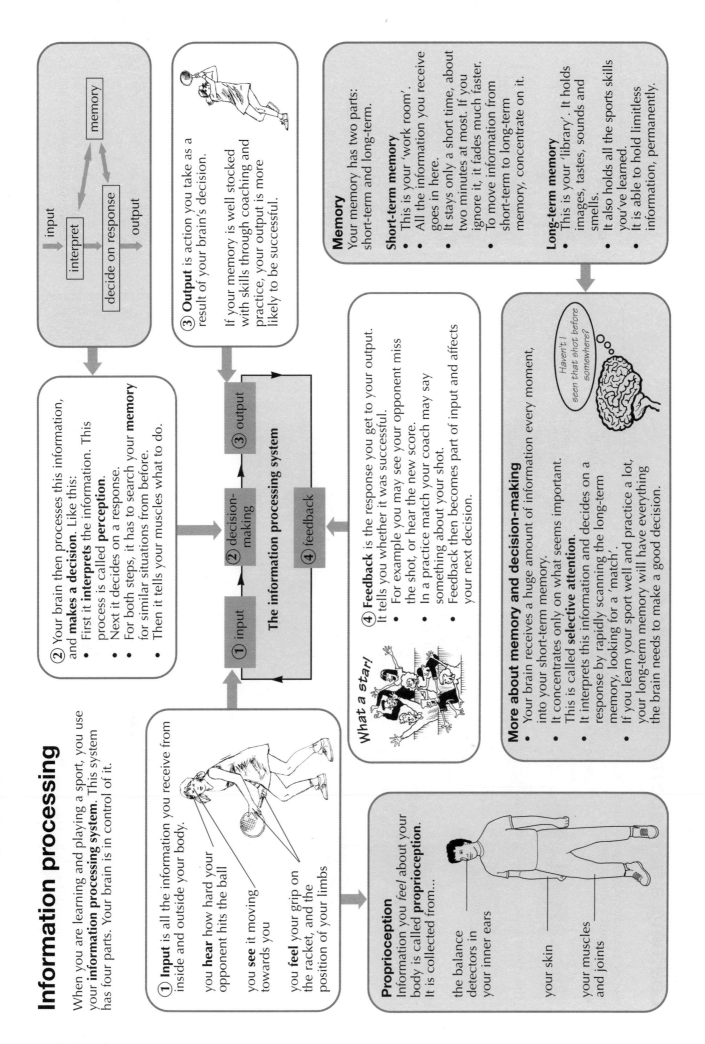

**input** → **interpret** → **decide on response** → **output** (with **memory** feeding back)

① **Input** is all the information you receive from inside and outside your body.

you **hear** how hard your opponent hits the ball

you **see** it moving towards you

you **feel** your grip on the racket, and the position of your limbs

② Your brain then processes this information, and **makes a decision**. Like this:
- First it **interprets** the information. This process is called **perception**.
- Next it decides on a response.
- For both steps, it has to search your **memory** for similar situations from before.
- Then it tells your muscles what to do.

③ **Output** is action you take as a result of your brain's decision.

If your memory is well stocked with skills through coaching and practice, your output is more likely to be successful.

**The information processing system**

① input
② decision-making
③ output
④ feedback

④ **Feedback** is the response you get to your output. It tells you whether it was successful.
- For example you may see your opponent miss the shot, or hear the new score.
- In a practice match your coach may say something about your shot.
- Feedback then becomes part of input and affects your next decision.

*What a star!*

## Proprioception

Information you *feel* about your body is called **proprioception**. It is collected from...

the balance detectors in your inner ears

your skin

your muscles and joints

## Memory

Your memory has two parts: short-term and long-term.

**Short-term memory**
- This is your 'work room'. All the information you receive goes in here.
- It stays only a short time, about two minutes at most. If you ignore it, it fades much faster.
- To move information from short-term to long-term memory, concentrate on it.

**Long-term memory**
- This is your 'library'. It holds images, tastes, sounds and smells.
- It also holds all the sports skills you've learned.
- It is able to hold limitless information, permanently.

*Haven't I seen that shot before somewhere?*

## More about memory and decision-making
- Your brain receives a huge amount of information every moment, into your short-term memory.
- It concentrates only on what seems important. This is called **selective attention**.
- It interprets this information and decides on a response by rapidly scanning the long-term memory, looking for a 'match'.
- If you learn your sport well and practice a lot, your long-term memory will have everything the brain needs to make a good decision.

Q2, page 83 >

# Learning a new sports skill

You use your information processing system to **learn** a skill as well as perform it.

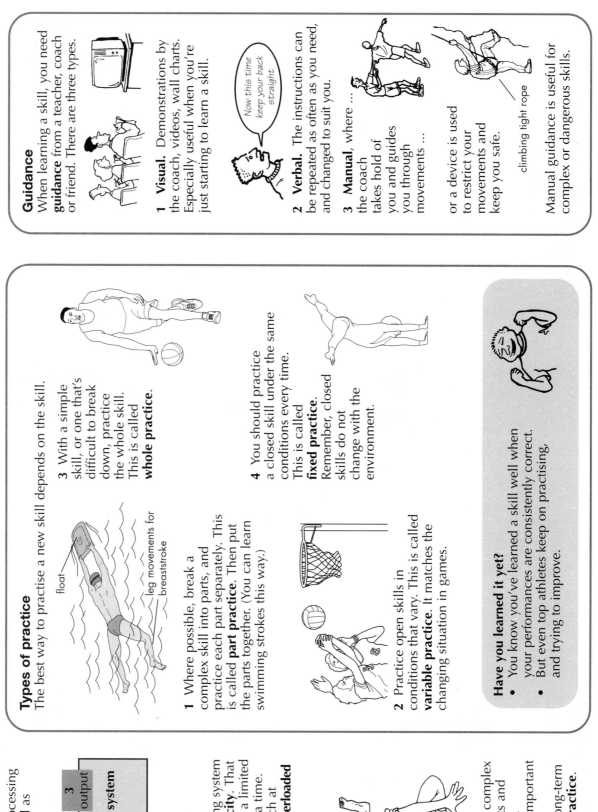

**1** input → **2** decision-making → **3** output

**4** feedback

**The information processing system**

## How to learn a new skill

- Your information processing system has **limited channel capacity**. That means it can process only a limited amount of information at a time.
- If you try to learn too much at once, the system will get **overloaded** and you'll feel confused.

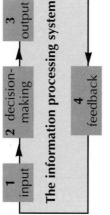

*I don't think this foot belongs to me!*

- So the best way to learn a complex skill is to break it into parts and learn each part separately.
- Concentrate on the most important aspects of the skill first.
- Move the skill into your long-term memory through lots of **practice**.

## Types of practice

The best way to practise a new skill depends on the skill.

*float*

*leg movements for breaststroke*

1 Where possible, break a complex skill into parts, and practice each part separately. This is called **part practice**. Then put the parts together. (You can learn swimming strokes this way.)

3 With a simple skill, or one that's difficult to break down, practice the whole skill. This is called **whole practice.**

2 Practice open skills in conditions that vary. This is called **variable practice**. It matches the changing situation in games.

4 You should practice a closed skill under the same conditions every time. This is called **fixed practice**. Remember, closed skills do not change with the environment.

### Have you learned it yet?

- You know you've learned a skill well when your performances are consistently correct.
- But even top athletes keep on practising, and trying to improve.

## Guidance

When learning a skill, you need **guidance** from a teacher, coach or friend. There are three types.

1 **Visual.** Demonstrations by the coach, videos, wall charts. Especially useful when you're just starting to learn a skill.

*Now this time keep your back straight*

2 **Verbal.** The instructions can be repeated as often as you need, and changed to suit you.

3 **Manual,** where ... the coach takes hold of you and guides you through movements ...

or a device is used to restrict your movements and keep you safe.

*climbing tight rope*

Manual guidance is useful for complex or dangerous skills.

Q3, page 83

# The importance of feedback

**Feedback** is the response you get to your **performance** or **output**. There are two kinds.

## Knowledge of performance (KP)

This tells you how well or badly you *performed*. You can obtain KP:
- from a coach, teacher, or friends.
- through proprioception, to some extent. This is called **internal** feedback. (You can *feel* how well you hit the ball.)
- by studying a video of your performance.

## Knowledge of results (KR)

This tells you whether you got the *result* you wanted. You can obtain KR:
- by looking. You see the football fly into the net.
- by listening or watching for the score.
- through proprioception, sometimes. You *know* when you land correctly from a somersault.

## The full picture
- You can perform badly but win (if your opponents were worse).
- You can perform well but lose ( (if your opponents were better).
- So you need both KP and KR to get the full picture.

## The four principles of feedback
1 Feedback is essential for improvement. (Both KP and KR.)
2 It should be given as soon as possible after the performance. (Otherwise you forget.)
3 It should be clear and to the point, so you know what to do next time.
4 You must have enough time to think it over before the next attempt.

## How can feedback help you?

Talking over your performance with a teacher or coach will help you to …
- identify your strengths so that you can build on them.
- identify weaknesses to work on.
- see if extra training or practice is needed.
- set goals for improvement.
- stay motivated.

*Cool!*

## Feedback, guidance and coaching

*coaching*
*setting goals*
*encouragement*
*feedback*
*guidance*
*planning*

- Feedback and guidance go hand in hand. They are both part of the job of coaching.
- Coaching plays a huge part in an athlete's success.
- The higher the level of the athlete, the better qualified the coach needs to be.
- But many young athletes get excellent coaching from unqualified coaches.

Who does the coaching?

personal top coach
national coach
team coach
teacher
family

level of athlete

Q4, page 83

# Factors affecting your performance

How well you perform in an event – dance, gymnastics, athletics or any other sport – depends on a variety of factors.

## Body factors (physiological)

1 **Skill.** The more skilful you are, the more likely you are to perform well.

2 **Fitness.** The fitter you are, the better.

3 **Physique.** You will perform better in an activity that suits your build or somatotype.

4 **Age.** If an activity depends on strength and speed, you'll perform better at 25 than 45. But for some activities (such as golf), age can be less important than experience.

5 **Body composition.** If you are overfat, you're carrying extra weight. Not good for your performance!

6 **Fatigue.** This reduces your skill level. Sufficient sleep is essential before a big event.

7 **Illness and injury.** Don't perform at all when you are ill or injured. An injury will get worse.

8 **Diet.** Diet affects your health, which in turn affects your fitness. What and when you eat *before* an event will also affect your performance. A heavy meal is not a good idea!

9 **Drugs.** Alcohol and cigarettes impair your performance. Some drugs do improve performance in the short term, but they damage your health in the long run. Athletes can be banned for using them.

## Mental factors (psychological)

1 **Personality.** Some sports suit some personalities better than others. You'll perform better in a sport that suits you!

2 **Motivation.** If you are keen to succeed, you are more likely to work hard and perform well.

3 **Arousal.** If you are too laid back, or too nervous, you won't perform as well as you could. You need to get psyched up to just the right level.

4 **Stress.** If you are feeling under stress for any reason, it is likely to impair your performance.

## Environmental factors

1 **The weather.** If it's hotter, colder, windier or more humid than you are used to, you won't perform as well as you could.

2 **Altitude.** At high altitudes, the air is 'thinner'. You take in less oxygen at each breath. If you're not used to this, it will make you feel breathless and dizzy.

3 **Pollution.** It harms your lungs, so your performance will be affected.

## Optimum performance

- Your body and mind affect each other.
- The environment can affect both.
- All three combine to produce your performance.
- If they're all at their best you'll give your optimum performance.

Q5, page 83

# Arousal in sport

**Arousal** is a state of excitement and alertness. You may reach a high level of arousal before a big event. These are all signs:

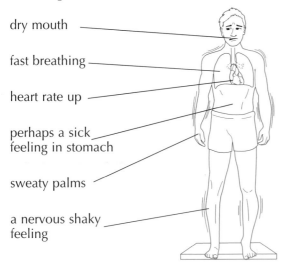

dry mouth

fast breathing

heart rate up

perhaps a sick feeling in stomach

sweaty palms

a nervous shaky feeling

## Increasing your arousal
All these help to increase arousal:
- a pep talk from your coach before an event
- the warm up before the event
- having a definite goal to achieve in the event
- bright lights and lots of noise around you
- friendly or hostile sports fans looking on.

But don't let yourself get over-aroused!

## Adrenaline and arousal
A hormone called **adrenaline** plays a big part in arousal.
- It is made by the **adrenal glands** just above your kidneys.
- When you are frightened or nervous, these glands squirt adrenaline into your blood.
- It has these effects:
  – it makes your heart beat faster, so more oxygen and glucose are pumped to the muscles.
  – it causes blood vessels in your gut and under your skin to constrict, shunting more blood to the muscles.
  – it makes your muscles tense, ready for action.
- So your heart thumps. Your stomach feels hollow. Your muscles may shiver. You are ready for 'fight or flight'.

*GULP!*

## Arousal and performance
You need just the right level of arousal to do your best in a sports event. Look at this graph:

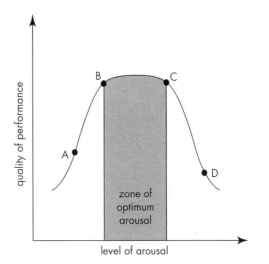

- At A, arousal is low. You may be feeling bored or tired. You are not 'psyched up' enough. You perform badly.
- Between B and C you are at optimum arousal. Your performance is at its best.
- If you are very anxious, your arousal level may rise to D. You are over-aroused or 'psyched out'. Your performance suffers.

This is called the **Inverted U Theory**.

## Preventing over-arousal
These techniques will stop you getting *too* nervous, before an event.
- **Relaxation.** Breathe slowly and deeply. Relax different muscle groups in turn.
- **Visualisation.** Go through the event in your mind in advance, in detail. 'See' yourself performing well and staying calm and confident.

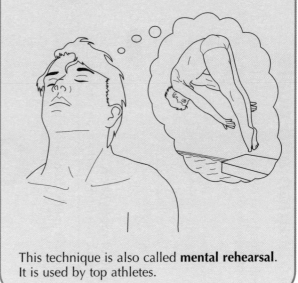

This technique is also called **mental rehearsal**. It is used by top athletes.

Q6, page 83

# Motivation and goals

**Motivation** is the driving force that makes you decide what to do, and how much effort to put in.

The more motivated you are ...
- the harder you will work at an activity
- the more likely you are to succeed.

## Types of motivation
There are two types, intrinsic and extrinsic.

**Intrinsic motivation** comes from the activity itself. You like it for its own sake.

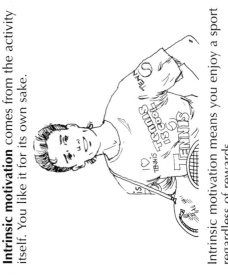

Intrinsic motivation means you enjoy a sport regardless of rewards.

- For most athletes, motivation is a mixture of intrinsic and extrinsic.
- Extrinsic motivation alone is dangerous, because when the rewards stop, so does the athlete!
- So coaches must make sure their athletes continue to enjoy the sport.

---

### Motivation and goals
A goal to aim for is a good motivator.

*Example of a sports goal: to perform a forward roll with my legs straight, at the next attempt.*

- A goal motivates you to work hard.
- It helps you prepare mentally for a performance, since you know what you're aiming for.
- It acts as a signpost, giving you direction in your training.
- It is something to check your progress against.
- Having a goal makes you feel less anxious, and more in control.
- Meeting a goal increases your confidence.

---

**Extrinsic motivation** comes from outside the activity. These are all **extrinsic motivators**:

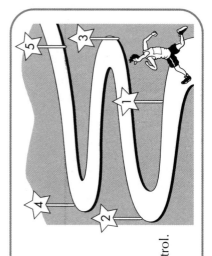

External motivators are useful, but have some disadvantages:
- If a reward is too difficult to obtain (or too easy), it may put you off.
- Competition for rewards may put you under too much pressure.
- You may lose interest in a sport if you fail to get a prize.

I'm giving up right this minute

---

### What makes a good goal?
Think **SMARTER!**

☆ **Specific.** 'I must run faster' is too vague. 'I must run 30 metres in under 4 seconds at my next attempt' is specific.

☆ **Measurable.** '30 metres in under 4 seconds' is a measurable goal. You can tell if you've met it.

☆ **Agreed.** You and your coach must agree about your goals. If you're not happy with them, they won't motivate you.

☆ **Realistic.** A goal that's too difficult will put you off.

☆ **Time-phased.** Goals should be mapped out for some time ahead, to give you direction. For example goals to be met in the next training session, by the end of next month, by the end of the year and so on.

☆ **Exciting.** Exciting, challenging goals stop you getting bored. As you progress they should get more difficult.

☆ **Recorded.** Goals should be written down. Then you know where you're going and can check your own progress.

Q7, page 83

# Aggression in sport

In sport, **aggression** can mean:
- acting forcefully *within the rules of the sport* to achieve your aim.
- acting with intent to cause harm to another player.

Here we concentrate on the first meaning.

## All athletes are aggressive

**Athlete** means any person playing serious sport.
*All* athletes show aggressive behaviour. But it's not always obvious! The more physical contact there is between players, the more obvious the aggression will be.

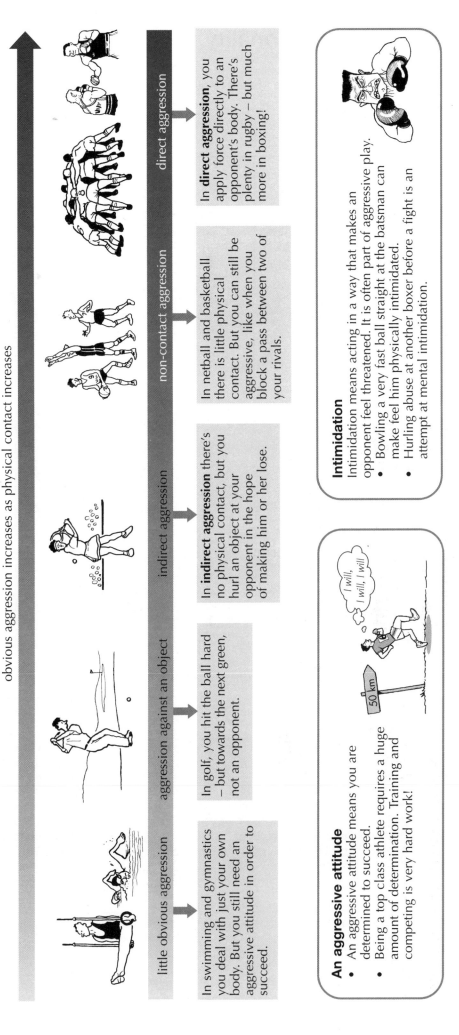

obvious aggression increases as physical contact increases

| little obvious aggression | aggression against an object | indirect aggression | non-contact aggression | direct aggression |
|---|---|---|---|---|

In swimming and gymnastics you deal with just your own body. But you still need an aggressive attitude in order to succeed.

In golf, you hit the ball hard – but towards the next green, not an opponent.

In **indirect aggression** there's no physical contact, but you hurl an object at your opponent in the hope of making him or her lose.

In netball and basketball there is little physical contact. But you can still be aggressive, like when you block a pass between two of your rivals.

In **direct aggression**, you apply force directly to an opponent's body. There's plenty in rugby – but much more in boxing!

### Aggression and injury
- Aggressive behaviour can cause injury, even within the rules.
- The more physical contact there is, the bigger the risk of injury. (Injury is part of boxing.)
- In a team game, it can be hard to tell whether an injury was caused by accident or on purpose.
- To reduce the risk of injury, coaches must encourage players to obey the rules and play cleanly.

### An aggressive attitude
- An aggressive attitude means you are determined to succeed.
- Being a top class athlete requires a huge amount of determination. Training and competing is very hard work!

I will, I will, I will

### Intimidation
Intimidation means acting in a way that makes an opponent feel threatened. It is often part of aggressive play.
- Bowling a very fast ball straight at the batsman can make feel him physically intimidated.
- Hurling abuse at another boxer before a fight is an attempt at mental intimidation.

Q8, page 83

# Sport and personality

Your **personality** is the set of characteristics that makes you you. Research suggests that personality affects your choice of sport or other activity, *and* the quality of your performance.

### Extroverts and introverts
One way to classify people is as **extrovert** or **introvert**.

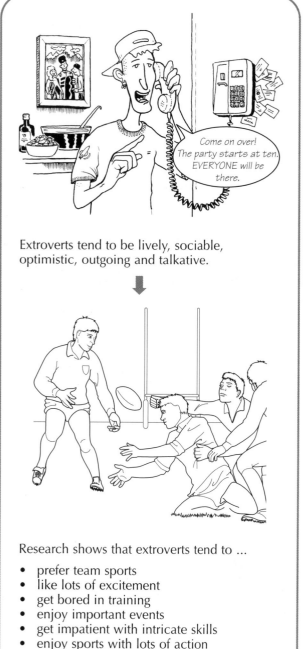

Extroverts tend to be lively, sociable, optimistic, outgoing and talkative.

Research shows that extroverts tend to ...

- prefer team sports
- like lots of excitement
- get bored in training
- enjoy important events
- get impatient with intricate skills
- enjoy sports with lots of action
- perform better at high levels of arousal
- enjoy contact sports
- have higher tolerance for pain.

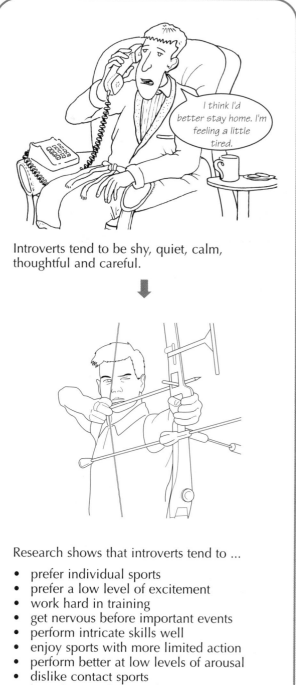

Introverts tend to be shy, quiet, calm, thoughtful and careful.

Research shows that introverts tend to ...

- prefer individual sports
- prefer a low level of excitement
- work hard in training
- get nervous before important events
- perform intricate skills well
- enjoy sports with more limited action
- perform better at low levels of arousal
- dislike contact sports
- have lower tolerance for pain.

- Beware. Don't label someone as extrovert or introvert until you have observed that person closely, in different situations. (A person who is very talkative with friends may appear quiet and shy with strangers.)
- The links between personality and sport above are generalisations. You will always find exceptions. For example, introverts who play team sports.
- There are also many other ways to classify personality.

Q9, page 83

# Alcohol, smoking, doping and sports performance

A **drug** is any chemical substance that affects the way your body works. Alcohol and cigarettes are examples! Most drugs affect sports performance in some way.

## Alcohol

*All* alcoholic drinks contain the chemical **ethanol**, which makes people 'drunk'.

It takes at least 1 hour for the body to recover from the effects of 1 unit of alcohol.

After heavy drinking, there is still alcohol in the blood next day.

Each contains 1 unit of alcohol:
½ pint of regular beer
1 glass of wine
1 pub measure of spirits

## Effects of alcohol on the body

- It affects co-ordination, judgement, balance, speech and hearing.
- It lowers the level of glycogen in muscles. So they can't work so long or hard.
- It leaves a 'hangover' which is partly dehydration.
- Athletes who drink too much lose their drive to train and compete.
- Long-term alcohol abuse leads to kidney and liver damage.

## Smoking

There is no 'safe' level of smoking. Every cigarette is dangerous. This is what you get when you inhale cigarette smoke...

**carbon monoxide**, a poisonous gas. In your lungs, red blood cells take it up instead of oxygen. So the blood now carries less oxygen to muscle fibres and other body cells. This will affect sports performance.

**nicotine,** an addictive poison. It makes the heart rate and blood pressure rise. It makes new smokers dizzy. It causes heart disease.

**tar**, a treacly brown substance. It collects in the lungs and breathing tubes. It clogs them and stops you breathing properly. This will affect sports performance. It also causes lung cancer and bronchitis.

## Doping

This means taking drugs to improve sporting performance. Athletes may take a drug:
- to pep up their performance
- to kill pain so that they can keep going
- to build muscles faster than they can do by training
- to calm themselves before big events.

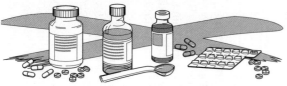

An athlete who dopes is cheating. Besides, most drugs were developed for medical use, and misuse damages the body. See next page for drugs that are banned in sport.

## Blood doping

The more red blood cells you have, the more oxygen reaches the muscles. This helps them work for longer.

In **blood doping**, an athlete withdraws blood a few weeks before a big event. The red cells are separated and frozen. Just before the event they are thawed and injected back into the athlete.

### Dangers

- All blood transfusions and injections carry a risk of infection.
- Top athletes already have a high concentration of red cells. Adding more may block their capillaries.

# Types of drugs banned by the International Olympic Committee

- Athletes representing their region or country, in any sport, can be tested at any time for these drugs.
- The tests are carried out on urine samples, at official labs.
- If a test proves positive, the athlete is banned from competition for at least a year.

## Beta blockers

These block the action of adrenaline, so that heart rate and breathing slow down. They are used to treat high blood pressure and heart disease. Some athletes misuse them to calm their nerves before big events.

*Dangers of misuse*
- Lower performance during lengthy events.
- Can cause sleep problems and depression.
- If blood pressure falls too low the user faints.

## Tranquillisers

These also reduce anxiety and calm you down. Examples are **Librium** and **Valium**.

*Dangers of misuse*
- The user feels dull and lacking in energy.
- They are addictive and hard to give up.

## Anabolic steroids

These build and repair muscle and bone. They include the male hormone **testosterone**. They occur naturally in the body, and are made artificially to treat wasting diseases.

Some athletes misuse them to increase the size and strength of muscles, and help them recover from training.

*Dangers of misuse*
Misuse of steroids causes many problems, including:
- heart disease and high blood pressure
- weakened ligaments and tendons
- infertility and cancer
- aggressive behaviour
- the growth of face and body hair, and deepening of the voice, in females.

## Stimulants

These pep you up. They include
- **amphetamines** such as Benzedrine and Dexedrine
- **caffeine**, found in tea and coffee.

They raise heart rate and blood pressure, speed up reactions, and suppress pain and fatigue. The athlete feels alert and confident, and can work hard for longer.

*Dangers of misuse*
- Pain and fatigue are the body's warning signals. If they are suppressed, an athlete carries on too long and risks cramps, strains, and overheating.
- The athlete feels really 'low' afterwards.
- Can cause aggressive behaviour.
- Heavy use leads to high blood pressure, and liver and brain damage.

## Narcotic analgesics

These kill pain, and give a feeling of well-being and drowsiness. They include:
- **heroin** and **morphine**
- **codeine**, a milder drug found in many painkillers and diarrhoea treatments.

*Dangers of misuse*
- Constipation and low blood pressure.
- They are addictive (even codeine).
- The withdrawal symptoms can be very unpleasant.
- Pain is a warning signal. Suppressing it can lead to further injury.
- Morphine and heroin are illegal in most countries except for medical use.

## Diuretics

These increase the amount of water excreted in urine. They are used for patients with heart disease who have too much body fluid. They are misused by:
- boxers and wrestlers who want to lose weight quickly before a weigh-in.
- other athletes who want to flush traces of banned drugs from their bodies.

*Dangers of misuse*
- Sodium and potassium salts get excreted as well as water. The body needs these salts.
- Low levels of potassium lead to muscle weakness and heart damage.

Q11, page 83

# Hygiene and foot care

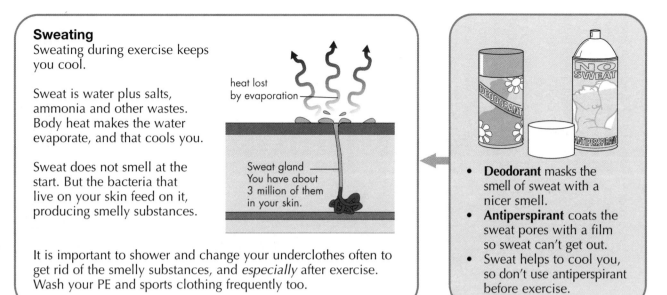

## Sweating

Sweating during exercise keeps you cool.

Sweat is water plus salts, ammonia and other wastes. Body heat makes the water evaporate, and that cools you.

Sweat does not smell at the start. But the bacteria that live on your skin feed on it, producing smelly substances.

It is important to shower and change your underclothes often to get rid of the smelly substances, and *especially* after exercise. Wash your PE and sports clothing frequently too.

heat lost by evaporation

Sweat gland
You have about 3 million of them in your skin.

- **Deodorant** masks the smell of sweat with a nicer smell.
- **Antiperspirant** coats the sweat pores with a film so sweat can't get out.
- Sweat helps to cool you, so don't use antiperspirant before exercise.

## Foot infections

These are two infections you can pick up in changing rooms.

|  | Athlete's foot | Veruccas |
|---|---|---|
| What it is | A **fungus** that grows between the toes, making the skin cracked and itchy. | Flat **warts** that grow on the soles of the feet. They are caused by a virus. |
| How it spreads | By direct contact. Also from socks, towels and wet changing room floors. | In the same way as athlete's foot. They are highly contagious. |
| How to avoid | Take care where you walk in bare feet. Use flip-flops in changing rooms and around swimming pools. Wash feet often and dry carefully between the toes. Avoid socks and shoes that make your feet sweaty. | Take care where you walk in bare feet. Use flip-flops in changing rooms and around swimming pools. |
| How to treat | Spray, powder or ointment from the chemist. | Ointment or pads from the chemist. |

## Corns, bunions and blisters

Shoes that are too tight can cause corns, bunions and blisters.

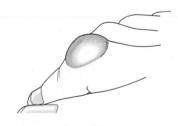

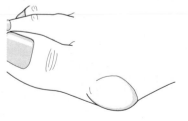

**Corns** are pads of thick hard skin that form on the toes and soles of feet. They can be very painful. Corn plasters may help, or go to a chiropodist.

At the joint of your big toe is a cushion of liquid called a **bursa**. If it gets inflamed the result is a **bunion**. Treatment for this means surgery.

Friction causes skin to **blister**. Don't burst a blister. If it does burst keep it clean and dry and cover it with gauze. Don't pick off the scab that forms.

Q12, page 83

# Preventing injury

## Two kinds of sports injury

- **Acute injuries** are the result of a sudden stress on the body.
  *Example*: a dislocated finger joint caused by a netball striking the finger.
- **Chronic** or **overuse injuries** are caused by:
  overtraining
  insufficient recovery time
  poor technique
  badly designed footwear or equipment.
  *Example*: tennis elbow.

## How to avoid acute injury

### Consider your body

1 Make sure you have practised the skills needed for the sport.
2 Know how to look after yourself during play, so that you avoid unnecessary risks.
3 Make sure you are fit for the activity. Don't take part if you are ill or injured.
4 Warm up correctly. There is less risk of muscle and joint injuries if you do.
5 Cool down correctly. This will prevent stiffness and soreness, so you are better prepared for the next event.

### Consider the event itself

1 Make sure you play at the right level for *you*. It can be dangerous to play against people who are bigger, stronger or more skilful.
2 Know the rules of the sport and obey them. They were developed to protect you as well as test your skill.
3 Pay attention to advice or warnings given by coaches, referees and other officials.

## How to avoid chronic injury

1 Make sure you develop the right techniques. For example, a poor throwing technique for the javelin leads to arm injury.
2 Choose kit and equipment carefully, and especially footwear.
3 Follow heavy training days with light days.
4 Even during hard training, take one day's rest a week.
5 Allow enough time for full recovery between training sessions and/or events.

## Consider kit and equipment

1 Make sure you are wearing the right kit. The right footwear is very important.
2 Don't forget things like mouth or shin guards if your sport requires them.
3 Don't wear jewellery or watches that could catch in clothing or equipment. Tie back long hair. For sports like netball, fingernails should be short.
4 Make sure the equipment is in good repair. For example no loose studs on rugby boots.
5 Lift large or heavy equipment with care. Poor lifting technique causes injury.

## Consider the environment

1 Watch out for hazards in the playing area – broken glass on pitches, wet patches on floors, rakes left in long jump pits.
2 Take special care in hazardous weather. Frost can make ground too hard. High winds and fog are dangers for canoeists. An event should be postponed if conditions are too hazardous.

## PE and the law

Schools have a duty to ensure safe practice in PE and sport, under the *Health and Safety at Work Act of 1974*. They must make sure that:

- safety equipment is available and working.
- first aid is available and emergency procedures are planned and followed.
- events and training sessions are properly planned and supervised.
- the group size suits the activity and the space available.
- the ability of the group matches the event.

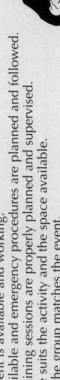

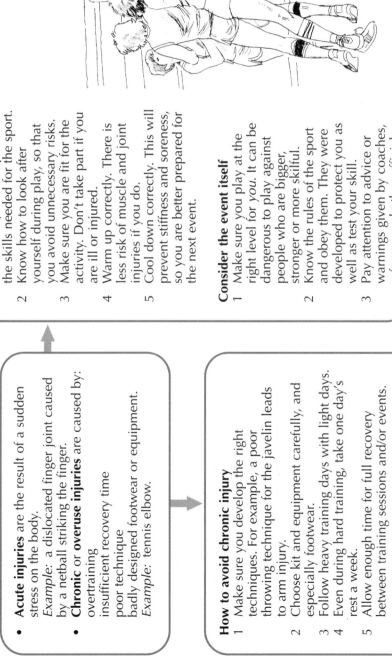

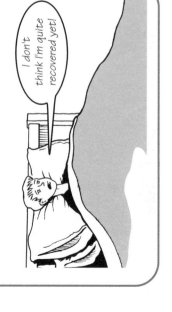

*I don't think I'm quite recovered yet!*

Q13, page 84 ▷

# Bone and joint injuries

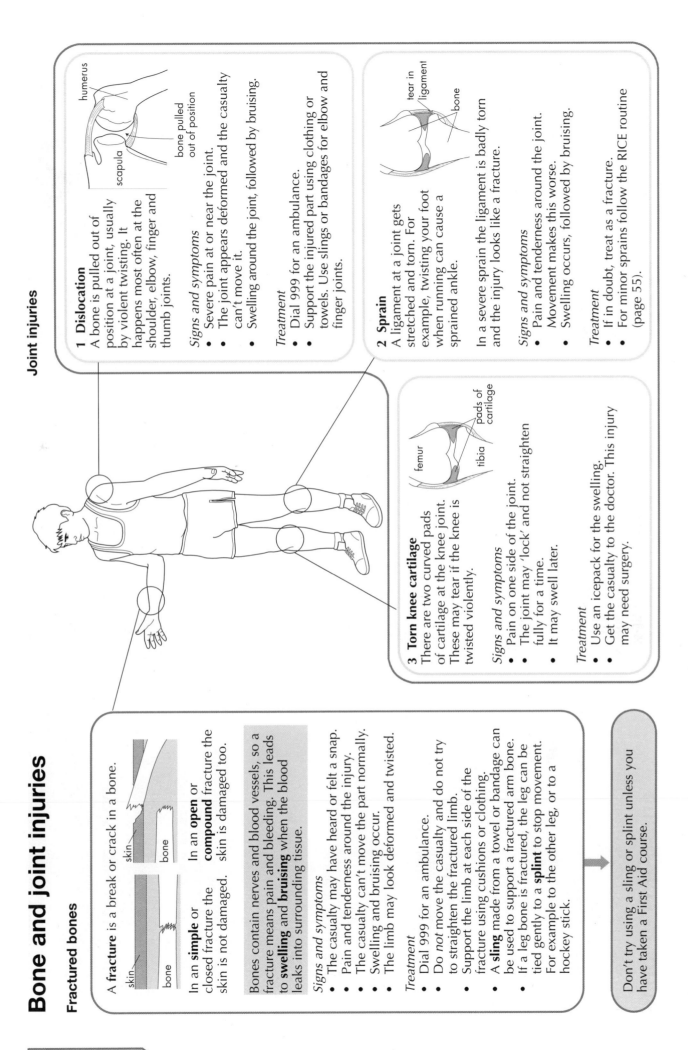

## Fractured bones

A **fracture** is a break or crack in a bone.

In an **simple** or closed fracture the skin is not damaged.

In an **open** or **compound** fracture the skin is damaged too.

Bones contain nerves and blood vessels, so a fracture means pain and bleeding. This leads to **swelling** and **bruising** when the blood leaks into surrounding tissue.

*Signs and symptoms*
- The casualty may have heard or felt a snap.
- Pain and tenderness around the injury.
- The casualty can't move the part normally.
- Swelling and bruising occur.
- The limb may look deformed and twisted.

*Treatment*
- Dial 999 for an ambulance.
- Do *not* move the casualty and do not try to straighten the fractured limb.
- Support the limb at each side of the fracture using cushions or clothing.
- A **sling** made from a towel or bandage can be used to support a fractured arm bone.
- If a leg bone is fractured, the leg can be tied gently to a **splint** to stop movement. For example to the other leg, or to a hockey stick.

Don't try using a sling or splint unless you have taken a First Aid course.

## 1 Dislocation

A bone is pulled out of position at a joint, usually by violent twisting. It happens most often at the shoulder, elbow, finger and thumb joints.

*Signs and symptoms*
- Severe pain at or near the joint.
- The joint appears deformed and the casualty can't move it.
- Swelling around the joint, followed by bruising.

*Treatment*
- Dial 999 for an ambulance.
- Support the injured part using clothing or towels. Use slings or bandages for elbow and finger joints.

## 2 Sprain

A ligament at a joint gets stretched and torn. For example, twisting your foot when running can cause a sprained ankle.

In a severe sprain the ligament is badly torn and the injury looks like a fracture.

*Signs and symptoms*
- Pain and tenderness around the joint. Movement makes this worse.
- Swelling occurs, followed by bruising.

*Treatment*
- If in doubt, treat as a fracture.
- For minor sprains follow the RICE routine (page 55).

## 3 Torn knee cartilage

There are two curved pads of cartilage at the knee joint. These may tear if the knee is twisted violently.

*Signs and symptoms*
- Pain on one side of the joint.
- The joint may 'lock' and not straighten fully for a time.
- It may swell later.

*Treatment*
- Use an icepack for the swelling.
- Get the casualty to the doctor. This injury may need surgery.

# Injury to soft tissue

Your muscles and skin are **soft tissue**. These are the main injuries that occur.

## Injury to muscles

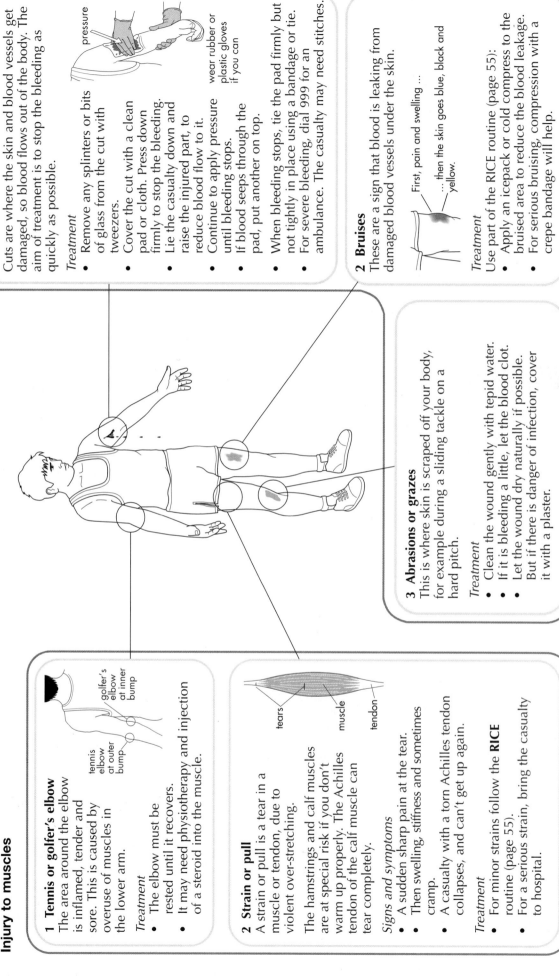

### 1 Tennis or golfer's elbow

The area around the elbow is inflamed, tender and sore. This is caused by overuse of muscles in the lower arm.

tennis elbow at outer bump

golfer's elbow at inner bump

*Treatment*
- The elbow must be rested until it recovers.
- It may need physiotherapy and injection of a steroid into the muscle.

### 2 Strain or pull

A strain or pull is a tear in a muscle or tendon, due to violent over-stretching.

tears

muscle

tendon

The hamstrings and calf muscles are at special risk if you don't warm up properly. The Achilles tendon of the calf muscle can tear completely.

*Signs and symptoms*
- A sudden sharp pain at the tear.
- Then swelling, stiffness and sometimes cramp.
- A casualty with a torn Achilles tendon collapses, and can't get up again.

*Treatment*
- For minor strains follow the **RICE** routine (page 55).
- For a serious strain, bring the casualty to hospital.

# Injury to skin

### 1 Cuts

Cuts are where the skin and blood vessels get damaged, so blood flows out of the body. The aim of treatment is to stop the bleeding as quickly as possible.

pressure

wear rubber or plastic gloves if you can

*Treatment*
- Remove any splinters or bits of glass from the cut with tweezers.
- Cover the cut with a clean pad or cloth. Press down firmly to stop the bleeding.
- Lie the casualty down and raise the injured part, to reduce blood flow to it.
- Continue to apply pressure until bleeding stops.
- If blood seeps through the pad, put another on top.
- When bleeding stops, tie the pad firmly but not tightly in place using a bandage or tie.
- For severe bleeding, dial 999 for an ambulance. The casualty may need stitches.

### 2 Bruises

These are a sign that blood is leaking from damaged blood vessels under the skin.

First, pain and swelling ...

... then the skin goes blue, black and yellow.

*Treatment*

Use part of the RICE routine (page 55):
- Apply an icepack or cold compress to the bruised area to reduce the blood leakage.
- For serious bruising, compression with a crepe bandage will help.

### 3 Abrasions or grazes

This is where skin is scraped off your body, for example during a sliding tackle on a hard pitch.

*Treatment*
- Clean the wound gently with tepid water.
- If it is bleeding a little, let the blood clot.
- Let the wound dry naturally if possible. But if there is danger of infection, cover it with a plaster.

Q16, page 84

# The RICE routine

The purpose of the **RICE routine** is to reduce pain, swelling and bruising around an injured part, and speed up the healing process.

**Pain, swelling and bruising**

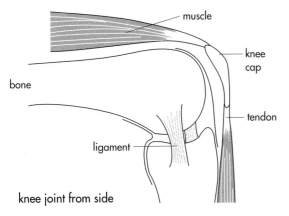

knee joint from side

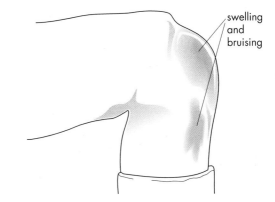

When bones, joints, ligaments, muscles or tendons get damaged, the blood vessels around them get damaged too.

The blood leaks into the surrounding tissue, causing pain, swelling and bruising. The leaked blood also slows down healing.

RICE works by reducing the amount of blood that leaks.

**R**est
**I**ce
**C**ompression
**E**levation

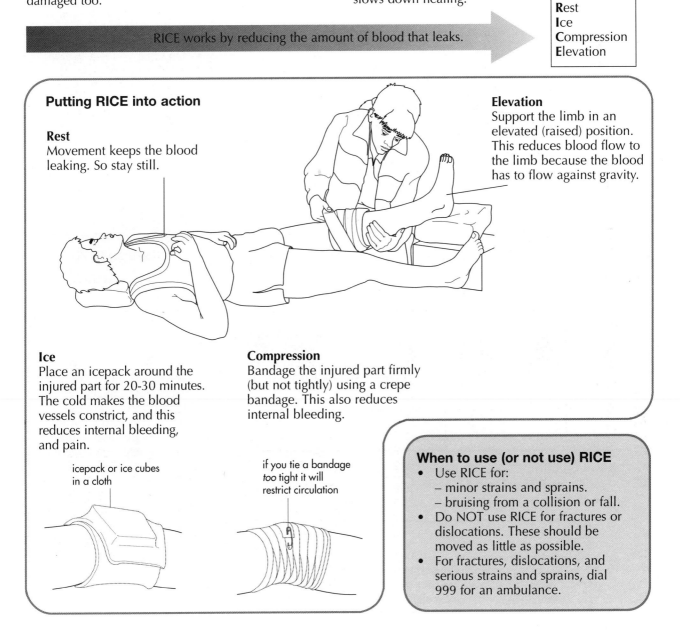

**Putting RICE into action**

**Rest**
Movement keeps the blood leaking. So stay still.

**Elevation**
Support the limb in an elevated (raised) position. This reduces blood flow to the limb because the blood has to flow against gravity.

**Ice**
Place an icepack around the injured part for 20-30 minutes. The cold makes the blood vessels constrict, and this reduces internal bleeding, and pain.

icepack or ice cubes in a cloth

**Compression**
Bandage the injured part firmly (but not tightly) using a crepe bandage. This also reduces internal bleeding.

if you tie a bandage *too* tight it will restrict circulation

**When to use (or not use) RICE**
- Use RICE for:
  – minor strains and sprains.
  – bruising from a collision or fall.
- Do NOT use RICE for fractures or dislocations. These should be moved as little as possible.
- For fractures, dislocations, and serious strains and sprains, dial 999 for an ambulance.

Q17, page 84

# The DRABC routine

This is what to do when a person has collapsed, and may be unconscious. The aim is to keep the **casualty** (injured person) breathing until an ambulance arrives. Lack of oxygen very quickly leads to brain damage.

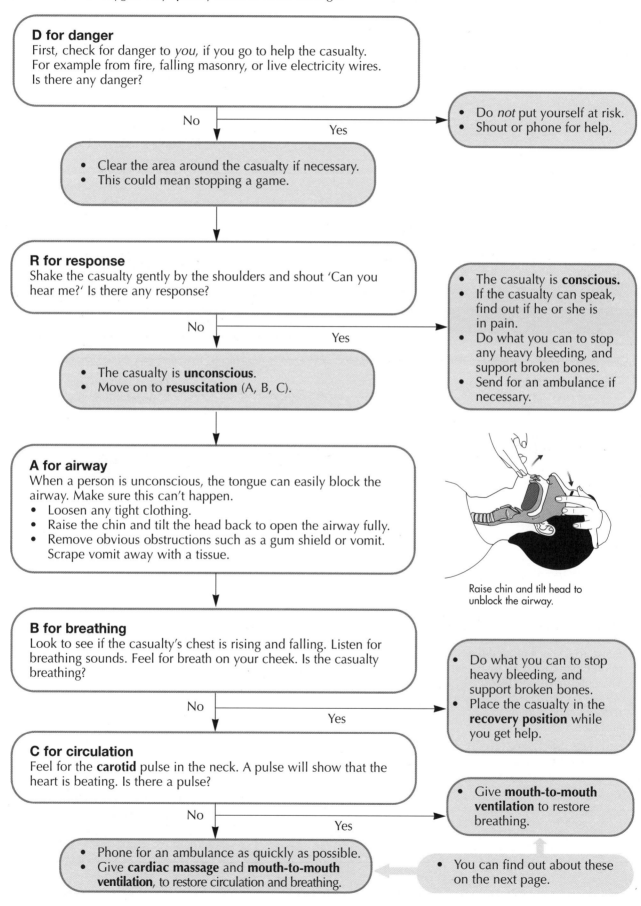

**D for danger**
First, check for danger to *you*, if you go to help the casualty. For example from fire, falling masonry, or live electricity wires. Is there any danger?

No          Yes

- Do *not* put yourself at risk.
- Shout or phone for help.

- Clear the area around the casualty if necessary.
- This could mean stopping a game.

**R for response**
Shake the casualty gently by the shoulders and shout 'Can you hear me?' Is there any response?

No          Yes

- The casualty is **conscious.**
- If the casualty can speak, find out if he or she is in pain.
- Do what you can to stop any heavy bleeding, and support broken bones.
- Send for an ambulance if necessary.

- The casualty is **unconscious**.
- Move on to **resuscitation** (A, B, C).

**A for airway**
When a person is unconscious, the tongue can easily block the airway. Make sure this can't happen.
- Loosen any tight clothing.
- Raise the chin and tilt the head back to open the airway fully.
- Remove obvious obstructions such as a gum shield or vomit. Scrape vomit away with a tissue.

Raise chin and tilt head to unblock the airway.

**B for breathing**
Look to see if the casualty's chest is rising and falling. Listen for breathing sounds. Feel for breath on your cheek. Is the casualty breathing?

No          Yes

- Do what you can to stop heavy bleeding, and support broken bones.
- Place the casualty in the **recovery position** while you get help.

**C for circulation**
Feel for the **carotid** pulse in the neck. A pulse will show that the heart is beating. Is there a pulse?

No          Yes

- Give **mouth-to-mouth ventilation** to restore breathing.

- Phone for an ambulance as quickly as possible.
- Give **cardiac massage** and **mouth-to-mouth ventilation**, to restore circulation and breathing.

- You can find out about these on the next page.

Q18, page 84

# The DRABC routine *continued*

## Mouth-to-mouth ventilation

In **mouth-to-mouth ventilation** or **the kiss of life**, you force air from your lungs into the casualty's. The oxygen in it keeps the casualty alive.

1   Make sure the casualty's airway is fully open. Then pinch the nostrils closed with your thumb and first finger.

2   Take a deep breath. Seal your lips firmly around the casualty's open mouth. Breathe out smoothly and firmly until the chest rises.

3   Take your mouth away and breathe in. The chest will fall. Repeat with 1 breath every 6 seconds, for one minute.

- If breathing has not returned within a minute, phone 999 for an ambulance.
- Continue mouth-to-mouth ventilation until breathing returns or help arrives.
- Check the pulse once a minute. Be ready to do cardiac massage if needed.
- If breathing returns to normal, place the casualty in the recovery position.

**!** DO NOT try mouth-to-mouth ventilation if you don't have First Aid training.

## Cardiac massage

**Cardiac massage** or **external chest compression** is a way of forcing a stopped heart to beat. It must be combined with mouth-to-mouth ventilation so that the blood gets oxygen too.

X2

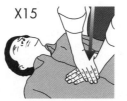
X15

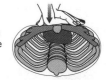
compression squeezes the heart

1   Make sure the casualty's airway is open. Do 2 breaths of mouth-to-mouth ventilation.

2   Now compress the chest 15 times as shown. Work smoothly and quickly, a bit faster than one compression per second.

3   Repeat this pattern of 2 ventilations and 15 compressions until help arrives or the casualty's condition improves.

- If the casualty moves, or the skin colour improves, check the pulse.
- If there is a pulse, but no breathing, continue with mouth-to-mouth ventilation. Check the pulse every minute.
- If breathing also restarts, place the casualty in the recovery position. Check the breathing and pulse every three minutes.

**!** DO NOT try cardiac massage if you don't have First Aid training.

## The recovery position

- This is the safest position for an unconscious breathing person.
- The head is tilted so that the tongue can't block the throat and the person can't choke on vomit.
- You can leave an unconscious person in this position while you get help.

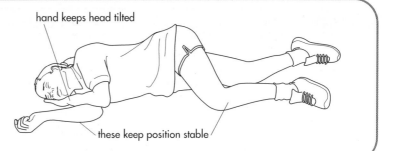

hand keeps head tilted

these keep position stable

Q19, page 84

# Cramp, concussion and other conditions

| Name | What it is | Signs and symptoms | Treatment |
|---|---|---|---|
| **Cramp** | It happens when muscle fibres fail to relax and their blood supply is cut off. | Pain in the muscle, often severe. (Usually in leg or foot muscles.) | • Stretch the muscle slowly and gently. Hold the stretch.<br>• When the muscle has relaxed, massage it gently. |
| **Stitch** | A small sharp pain in your side or upper abdomen. | Occurs during vigorous exercise. | Stop exercising for a short time and it will go. |
| **Concussion** | Caused by a blow to the head, which shakes the brain around. The symptoms may not appear until hours after the injury. | The casualty:<br>• may become unconscious, briefly or for hours.<br>• is confused, stares, and may suffer memory loss.<br>• feels sick, dizzy or drowsy. | • Place an unconscious person in the recovery position and dial 999 for an ambulance.<br>• Other casualties should be kept under observation for at least 24 hours. |
| **Shock** | Not enough blood is circulating round the body. This could be due to:<br>• fluid loss (as in severe bleeding or diarrhoea)<br>• severe pain, when blood is diverted to the painful part. | • Cold, clammy skin and blue lips.<br>• Rapid shallow breathing and a rapid weak pulse.<br>• The casualty feels dizzy, thirsty, anxious, panicky, and may try to vomit.<br>• The casualty may fall unconscious and die if fluid loss continues. | • Dial 999 for an ambulance.<br>• Do what you can to stop any heavy bleeding.<br>• Place the casualty in the recovery position.<br>• Reassure the casualty. Shock is very frightening. |
| **Hypothermia** | The body is too cold to function properly. Its core temperature has fallen below about 35°C.<br><br>The casualty may fall unconscious and die if not treated. | • Pale cold skin and shallow breathing.<br>• The casualty is weak and stumbles a lot.<br>• The casualty starts acting strangely, for example dreamy or aggressive.<br>• He or she has an overwhelming urge to lie down and rest. | • Bring the casualty into shelter, put into warm dry clothing and allow to rest.<br>• Then give a hot bath and hot sweet drinks. *No alcohol!*<br>• If there's no shelter, lie the casualty on blankets or other insulation and cover well.<br>• If the condition gets worse, send for help. |
| **Dehydration** | Too much water and salts lost in sweat. | The casualty feels weak and dizzy. | Give plenty of water to drink. |
| **Heat exhaustion** | Like dehydration but more severe. Both conditions may be caused by hard exercise on a hot day. | • Pale, grey, clammy skin.<br>• Weak, rapid pulse.<br>• The casualty feels weak and dizzy and may get cramps and headache.<br>• If water loss is severe, shock may develop. | • Lie the casualty down in a cool place, with legs raised.<br>• Give him or her frequent sips of a weak solution of salt in water.<br>• Call a doctor for further advice. |
| **Heat stroke** | The body suddenly stops sweating. Its temperature rises out of control. This usually happens during long, hard exercise on a hot, *humid* day. | • The casualty is flushed, with a rapid strong pulse and hot dry skin.<br>• He or she suddenly lapses into confusion or delirium.<br>• He or she may become unconscious and die if not treated quickly. | • Lie the casualty down in a cool breezy place. Remove outer clothing and wrap in a cold wet sheet.<br>• Keep the sheet saturated with cold water, and fan it continually until the casualty has cooled down.<br>• Call a doctor for further advice. |

Q20, page 84

# Leisure, recreation, and sport

leisure 3h
chores 1h
homework 2h
sleeping 9h
school 6.5h
travel 1h
eating 1.5h

Walkies!

**Leisure** is your free time, when you can do as you wish. What you choose will depend on your culture and upbringing, your friends, how much money you have, and so on.

**Recreation** is an activity you do just for pleasure, in your leisure time. It lets you recharge your batteries or **re-create** yourself. So you can cope better with stress.

In **physical recreation** the activity is a physical one, like cycling, football, swimming or rollerblading. (It does not include serious sport!)

## The **growth in leisure**
Over the last 50 or 60 years there has been a growth in leisure, because:

Machines have taken over many jobs at work. So more people are unemployed, or in part-time work, or forced to take early retirement.

They've also taken over many household chores, leaving more free time.

Better health care and a better standard of living means we live longer now. So there are more active, elderly people around.

## Why choose physical recreation?
There are three kinds of reason.

Why oh why?

- **Exercise.** You might take up jogging or swimming just to get more healthy and fit.
- **Enjoyment of the activity.** You might go sailing or jazz dancing just because you love it.
- **Social reasons.** If you join a club or team, you get the chance to meet new people and make new friends.
- So physical recreation can improve your physical, mental and social well-being. In other words, it's good for your health!

See next page for more.

## Providing for leisure
- The growth in leisure means the **leisure industry** is booming.
- It provides cinemas, ice rinks, theme parks, package holidays and so on, in order to make a **profit**.
- Some facilities are provided by **local authorities**: swimming pools, parks and so on. Their aim is to serve the local people rather than make a profit.
- Voluntary organizations like the National Trust and the Youth Hostel Association also provide leisure facilities.

Page 62 has more about facilities.

## Where does sport fit in?
Sport has three characteristics.
- It is **institutionalised** and **competitive**. That means there are organized events with rules and regulations, and you set out to win.
- It calls for vigorous physical exertion or the use of complex skills. Lazing in a pool does not count.
- The player is motivated by enjoyment *plus other factors* such as payment or a prize. He or she may even earn a living from it.

You can show physical recreation and sport on a continuum. Take swimming as an example:

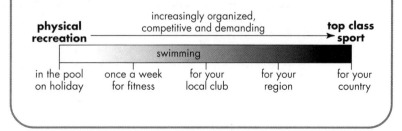

physical recreation

increasingly organized, competitive and demanding

top class sport

swimming

in the pool on holiday | once a week for fitness | for your local club | for your region | for your country

# The benefits from sport and physical recreation

Sport and physical recreation bring physical, mental *and* social benefits.

## Physical benefits

If an activity is strenuous enough, and you do it regularly enough, you will look and feel better.

The heart-lung team gets more efficient at delivering oxygen, so you don't get tired so easily.

Muscles get stronger and contract more efficiently.

When back and abdomen muscles get 'toned up' in this way, your **posture** improves.

Body fat gets burned up faster, so your shape improves.

Joints grow more flexible so you move more smoothly and easily.

Bones get stronger. The extra stress on them makes bone cells work harder.

## Mental benefits

- A lively game or work-out is stimulating and fun.
- It relieves stress and tension, and gets rid of aggression in a harmless way.
- It provides a challenge for you. You won't be bored.
- You forget your problems, and later they won't seem quite so serious.
- You'll sleep better afterwards, so you'll feel better rested.
- If you are good at an activity, it boosts your self-confidence.

## Social benefits

- Taking up a sport or physical recreation often means joining a team or club.
- You meet people with the same interest, and make new friends.
- In a team, you develop a spirit of teamwork and co-operation. This is useful in your working life.
- If you are talented at your activity, you might be able to turn it into a career.

## It all adds up to better health

- Health is a state of physical, mental and social well-being.
- Sport and physical recreation benefit you in all these areas. So they are good for your health!
- Research shows that a regularly active person runs less risk of heart disease, high blood pressure, back pain and cancers.

## More about posture

- **Good posture** means holding your body in the way that puts *least strain* on muscles, bones and joints.
- If you have poor posture, the extra strain on your body makes you tired sooner. It can also lead to back pain, fallen arches and other problems.
- Poor posture means a greater risk of sports injuries.
- Regular exercise will improve your posture.

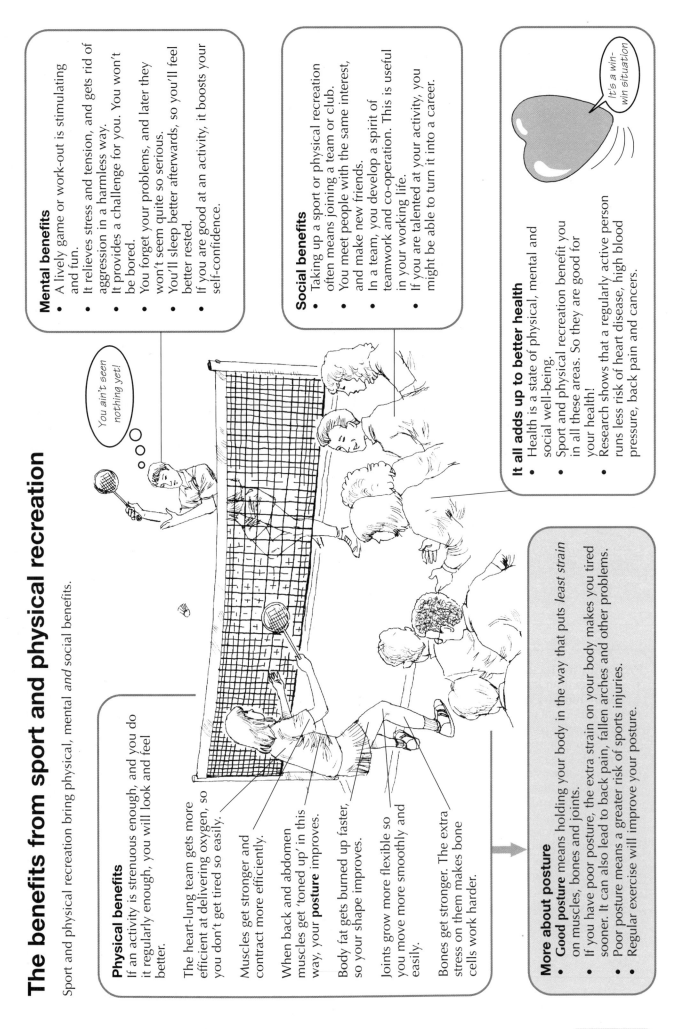

*You ain't seen nothing yet!*

*It's a win-win situation*

Q2, page 84

# Factors affecting participation in sport and physical recreation

Some people (and some countries) take part in more sport and physical recreation than others. It depends on all these factors.

**Economics.** Some activities (such as golf and riding) can be quite expensive. You might be unable to afford them. In the same way a city, area or country might not have the money to build sports facilities.

Unemployed people have plenty of time, but often not much money. So sports facilities often charge them less, especially at quiet times of day.

**Access.** The easier it is to get to a sports facility, the more likely you are to go there! If the nearest one is miles away, or even abroad, that makes participation difficult.

**Disability.** This will restrict the choice of activity. But many sports encourage disabled people, and modern sports centres have ramps for wheelchairs and special changing rooms.

**Environment and climate.** If you live near the sea or a lake it's easier to windsurf or sail. If you live in a cold climate it's easier to take up skiing.

**The media.** The media play a big part in making sport, exercise and fitness popular. By presenting an activity as exciting, trendy or fun, they encourage people to take part.

Sports can also go out of fashion. For example snooker and squash are less popular now than they were in the 1980s.

**Family.** You're more likely to take part in an activity if someone in the family encourages you. Most young people depend on a parent for money for kit, and help with travel to events.

**Peer-group pressure.** Your **peer group** is the group of people you associate with, who share your background and interests and are around your age. If your peer group takes part in an activity you are more likely to.

**Age.** People participate less as they get older. Only around 33% of 70-year-olds take some form of exercise (which might just be walking). Around 85% of 16-year-olds do.

The choice of activities also changes with age. Gymnastics and rugby aren't suitable if you are 70, but swimming, walking and crown green bowling are.

**Gender (sex).** Fewer females take part than males – around 57% of females compared with around 72% of males.

**Education.** If your school is strong on PE and sport, and you enjoy these at school, you are more likely to participate later.

**Tradition and culture.** These affect both the extent of participation and the choice of activity. For example:
- some cultures disapprove of women taking part in physical recreation in public, or in mixed company.
- some nations have a strong tradition in a sport – for example cricket in the West Indies and baseball in the USA.

**Politics.** The extent of participation also depends on politicians! For example a government could decide:
- to make everyone do PE at school.
- to pay towards the building of sports facilities for everyone.

Both would have a big effect on participation.

Q3, page 84

# Facilities for sport and physical recreation

Some facilities are **built** – for example gyms, swimming pools, tennis courts. Some are built indoors, some outdoors.

Others are **natural**: lakes, rivers, the sea, hills, forests and mountains. Like all facilities, they need to be looked after.

Some facilities are **multi-purpose**, with many different activities and users. Others cater for just one activity.

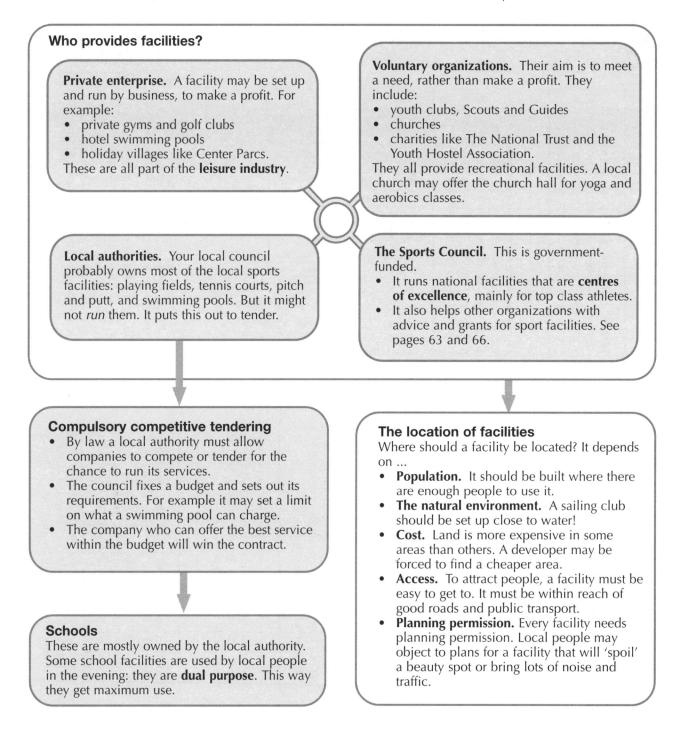

## Who provides facilities?

**Private enterprise.** A facility may be set up and run by business, to make a profit. For example:
- private gyms and golf clubs
- hotel swimming pools
- holiday villages like Center Parcs.

These are all part of the **leisure industry**.

**Voluntary organizations.** Their aim is to meet a need, rather than make a profit. They include:
- youth clubs, Scouts and Guides
- churches
- charities like The National Trust and the Youth Hostel Association.

They all provide recreational facilities. A local church may offer the church hall for yoga and aerobics classes.

**Local authorities.** Your local council probably owns most of the local sports facilities: playing fields, tennis courts, pitch and putt, and swimming pools. But it might not *run* them. It puts this out to tender.

**The Sports Council.** This is government-funded.
- It runs national facilities that are **centres of excellence**, mainly for top class athletes.
- It also helps other organizations with advice and grants for sport facilities. See pages 63 and 66.

### Compulsory competitive tendering
- By law a local authority must allow companies to compete or tender for the chance to run its services.
- The council fixes a budget and sets out its requirements. For example it may set a limit on what a swimming pool can charge.
- The company who can offer the best service within the budget will win the contract.

### The location of facilities
Where should a facility be located? It depends on ...
- **Population.** It should be built where there are enough people to use it.
- **The natural environment.** A sailing club should be set up close to water!
- **Cost.** Land is more expensive in some areas than others. A developer may be forced to find a cheaper area.
- **Access.** To attract people, a facility must be easy to get to. It must be within reach of good roads and public transport.
- **Planning permission.** Every facility needs planning permission. Local people may object to plans for a facility that will 'spoil' a beauty spot or bring lots of noise and traffic.

### Schools
These are mostly owned by the local authority. Some school facilities are used by local people in the evening: they are **dual purpose**. This way they get maximum use.

Q4, page 84

# Organizations for sport and physical recreation (I)

## The Sports Council

The Sports Council was set up by the government in 1972, with these aims:

1  to increase participation in sport and physical recreation
2  to increase the number and quality of facilities
3  to develop excellence in sport.

It is in fact organized as five separate councils:

- It is funded by the government (through the Department of National Heritage).
- But it acts as an independent body.

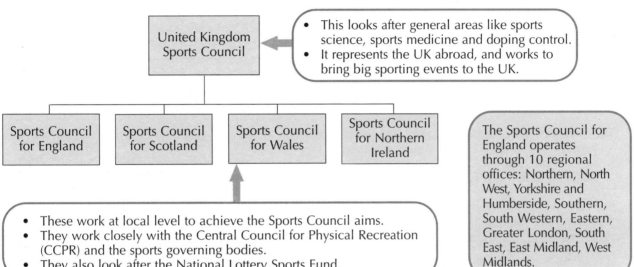

United Kingdom Sports Council

- This looks after general areas like sports science, sports medicine and doping control.
- It represents the UK abroad, and works to bring big sporting events to the UK.

Sports Council for England | Sports Council for Scotland | Sports Council for Wales | Sports Council for Northern Ireland

- These work at local level to achieve the Sports Council aims.
- They work closely with the Central Council for Physical Recreation (CCPR) and the sports governing bodies.
- They also look after the National Lottery Sports Fund.

The Sports Council for England operates through 10 regional offices: Northern, North West, Yorkshire and Humberside, Southern, South Western, Eastern, Greater London, South East, East Midland, West Midlands.

---

### What the Sports Council does to achieve its aims

#### 1  To increase participation

- In the past the Sports Council ran **campaigns** directed at different groups of people.
  For example the campaign **Sport for all disabled people** in 1981 encouraged disabled people to take up a sport, and encouraged facilities to provide them with better access.
- It now gives priority to **school sport**. If you play sport at school you are more likely to play later. So the Sports Council:
  – gives grants to teachers to take coaching courses.
  – gives grants for projects that link schools with local clubs.
  – encourages local businesses to sponsor school sports.

#### 2  To increase the number and quality of facilities

- It gives out grants from the Lottery Sports Fund for facilities and equipment (around £250 million a year).
- It gives advice on designing, building and running facilities.
- It designs and tests new kinds of facilities, such as new artificial playing surfaces.

#### 3  To develop excellence

Athletes need skill and determination to become top class.
They also need top coaching and facilities, and financial help.
So the Sports Council:
- runs the National Coaching foundation. (See page 66.)
- runs six National Centres for Excellence. (See page 66.)
- develops and co-ordinates sources of funding for athletes.

Of every £1 spent on a National Lottery ticket, 5.6p goes to the Lottery Sports Fund. This is handled by the Sports Council.

Q5, page 84

# Organizations for sport and physical recreation (II)

## The Central Council for Physical Recreation (CCPR)

This is an umbrella organization for over 270 governing bodies and associations for sport and physical recreation. Its aims are:
- to encourage participation in sport and physical recreation
- to represent and promote the interests of its members.

**It is funded by ...**
- donations from its members
- sponsorship from business
- sales of its publications
- a big Sports Council grant.

**The money is used to ...**
- tackle issues such as drugs in sport, sport for the disabled, and the 'unfair' taxation of sport
- provide legal and financial advice for members
- promote British sport abroad.

The members of the CCPR are divided into six groups:
- games and sports
- outdoor pursuits
- major spectator sports
- water recreation
- movement and dance
- interested organizations.

Each group elects a committee. The committee in turn elect the central committee that runs the CCPR.

*Some members of the CCPR...*
The British Horse Society
The British Judo Association
The Cyclists Touring Club
The Football Association
The Lawn Tennis Association

## National governing bodies

Each organized sport has a **national governing body.** The Football Association is an example. The governing body is responsible for:
- drawing up the rules of the sport and preventing their abuse
- organizing local and national competitions
- selecting teams for international competitions
- settling disputes within the sport
- managing and coaching referees and umpires
- helping to develop facilities
- maintaining links with sister governing bodies in other countries, and the European and World governing bodies

The national governing body is made up of regional or local governing bodies. These elect a central council to run the national governing body.

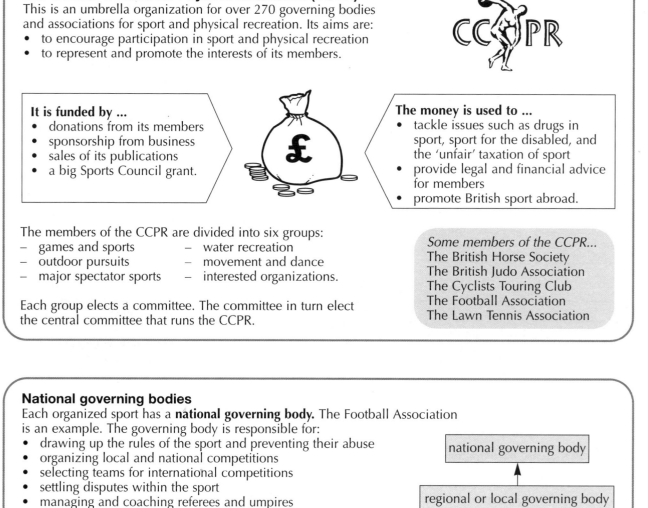

**They are funded by ...**
- ticket sales for major events
- members' subscriptions
- sponsorship
- Sports Council grants
- Lottery Sports Fund grants
- the sale of broadcast rights.

**The money is used to ...**
- manage the sport
- organize big events
- develop the sport
- maintain international links
- support clubs with grants
- run coaching schemes etc.

## Regional and local governing bodies

These represent the clubs in their areas. They act as a link between local clubs and the national governing body. For example:
- in swimming, England is divided into five regions. Each has a regional governing body.
- in rugby union, there are no regional governing bodies. Instead each county has a local governing body.

Q6, page 84

# Organizations for sport and physical recreation (III)

**The Sports Aid Foundation (SAF)**
Many promising athletes can't afford the expense of training and competing.
The SAF raises money to help these athletes.

**Money in from ...**
- sponsors
- donations from business, local authorities, voluntary bodies, the public.

**Money out as grants to ...**
- top athletes who are likely to win medals in the Olympics or World or European Championships.
- promising young athletes, and disabled athletes, to help them achieve their potential.

**The International Olympic Committee (IOC)**
This is the top committee of the Olympic Movement. It is chosen from member countries. Its main jobs are:
- to select the cities where the games will be held
- to decide which sports will be included
- to work with the host city and other bodies to plan the games
- to lead the fight against doping in sport.

**Money in from ...**
- sale of TV rights to the Olympic Games
- sponsorship by worldwide companies like Coca Cola.

**Money shared out between ...**
- the IOC
- the International Sports Federations
- the National Olympic Committees
- the Organizing Committee for each Olympics.

**The British Olympic Association (BOA)**
The BOA is part of the Olympic Movement. Its main jobs are:
- to select the British team for the Olympic Games
- to raise money to send the team to the games
- to make all the arrangements for getting it there
- to work with governing bodies to prepare the athletes.

**Money in from ...**
- the IOC
- sponsors
- licensing its logo (for T-shirts and so on)
- donations from the public.

**Money used for ...**
- selecting and preparing a team for the Games
- travel costs and living expenses for the athletes
- other expenses such as medical care
- Olympic kit for the athletes.

**The Countryside Commission (CC)**
It looks after the English countryside and advises the government on countryside matters. Its aim is to ensure that the countryside is enjoyed for physical recreation, but also protected.

**Money in from ...**
- the government, as a grant from the Department of the Environment.

**Money used to ...**
- develop National Trails like the Pennine Way for walkers, cyclists and riders
- restore public rights of way
- look after special parts of the countryside including the seven National Parks, the Heritage Coasts, and Areas of Outstanding Natural Beauty.

Q7, page 84

# Striving for excellence

To become a first-class athlete you need skill and determination. But success also depends on:

- coaching
- training facilities
- having the funds to train and compete
- input from sports science and sports medicine.

## The National Coaching Foundation (NCF)

This was set up by the Sports Council to improve coaching skills. It includes:

- the **Coach Development Unit**, which runs courses for coaches at all levels.
- 16 **National Coaching Centres**, based in universities and colleges round the UK. They run courses on behalf of governing bodies and other organizations.
- **Champion Coaching**, a scheme of after-school coaching for promising 11-14 year olds who are put forward by their PE teachers.

To improve coaching in schools, the Sports Council offers teachers grants to do coaching courses.

## Sports science and sports medicine

- Sports science studies the effect of things like training methods, diet and rest on an athlete's performance.
- Sports medicine deals with the treatment of sports injuries.
- The United Kingdom Sports Council has responsibility for these areas.
- It has a network of sports scientists who advise governing bodies, and help to prepare top athletes for major events.
- The National Sports Medicine Institute is a similar network of medical experts with special interest in sport.

## Centres of excellence

The UK has six **centres of excellence** for sport. They are funded and run by the Sports Council, and provide top class facilities, coaching and accommodation for athletes.

1. **Crystal Palace** for athletics, swimming, boxing, martial arts and judo. It also serves as a national and international venue for these sports.
2. **Bisham Abbey** for tennis. It also caters for football, hockey, squash, weight training and golf.
3. **Lilleshall** for football. It also caters for table tennis, cricket, gymnastics, archery, hockey and other sports, and has a sports injuries clinic.
4. **Holme Pierrepoint** for water sports.
5. **Plas-Y-Brenin** in Wales for outdoor activities, including climbing, canoeing, orienteering and dry-slope skiing.
6. The **National Cycling Centre** for cycling.

The centres are used mainly by governing bodies to run training programmes and events for their athletes. But they also cater for other users, including complete beginners.

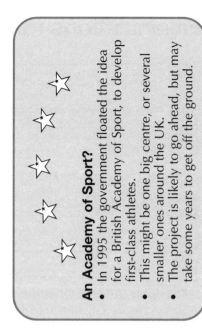

### An Academy of Sport?

- In 1995 the government floated the idea for a British Academy of Sport, to develop first-class athletes.
- This might be one big centre, or several smaller ones around the UK.
- The project is likely to go ahead, but may take some years to get off the ground.

## Funding

For promising athletes, training and competing can be a major expense.

- The Sports Aid Foundation (page 65) provides grants for some.
- Some manage to find a sponsor (page 72). Many have to work hard to fund themselves, which leaves less time for training.
- The Sports Council is now working to develop and co-ordinate all the sources of funding.

Q8, page 84

# Finance in sport

This shows how money is raised for sport, and how it is spent.

**Money in from ...**

**The government.** It raises money from **taxes**. Some goes to sport, through the Department of National Heritage. The Sports Council gets most of it – around £47 million a year.

**Local councils.** They raise money from local taxes, and spend some of it on facilities like swimming pools, playing fields and school gyms.

**The National Lottery.** This raises about £250 million a year for sport (5.6p from each ticket). The money goes into the Lottery Sports Fund and is given out as grants by the Sports Council.

**TV and radio.** These pay the governing bodies of sport for the right to broadcast sports events. In 1995 BSkyB agreed to pay £40 million a year, for 5 years, for Premier League football matches.

**Sponsorship.** Companies give money or other help to athletes, teams or events. Rover sponsors the tennis school at Bisham Abbey. IBM and CocaCola sponsor the Olympics.

**Private individuals.** Wealthy people may finance their favourite clubs, or even buy them! Blackburn Rovers is owned by the millionaire Jack Walker.

**Tickets and merchandise.** Clubs sell tickets to events, and replica strips, scarves, flags and so on. Big clubs can earn a lot this way.

**Membership and booking fees.** These are charged by golf and squash clubs, for example.

**Money out for ...**

- developing the sport
- building and improving facilities
- training athletes at all levels
- training coaches, referees, umpires
- running events of all sizes
- the salaries of paid officials and other employees
- the salaries of professional players
- prize money
- sports scholarships
- day to day running expenses (heating, lighting and so on)
- payments to shareholders, where a club is a public limited company or plc (like Manchester United)

### More about taxes
The government raises these taxes:
- **income tax** paid by individuals, as a percentage of their income.
- **corporation tax** paid by businesses, as a percentage of their profits.
- **Value added tax** (VAT), which is included in the price of most goods.
- **a gambling tax** on all money spent on gambling. Of each £1 bet on a horse race or football game, 6p is tax. For a £1 lottery ticket, 12p is tax.

The local council raises money through:
- **a council tax** on each household
- **a business tax** on local businesses.

Paying taxes can feel painful. But they pay for the running of the country – schools, the police, hospitals and so on.

### How the government earns from sport
It makes money *from* sport through:
- the corporation tax paid by sports bodies and companies in the sports business (for example equipment manufacturers).
- the income tax paid by individuals working in sport.
- the VAT paid on sports goods.
- the tax on gambling, including the Football Pools and horse racing.

It earns *much more* from sport than it gives back!

### The Lottery Sports Fund
Some people object to the National Lottery because it is gambling, and because many people who buy tickets can't really afford to.

However it does provide lots of money for sport. This is given as grants to sports projects which:
- will benefit the community.
- are well thought out and likely to succeed.
- can raise part of the cost from elsewhere.

Q9, page 84

# Inside a sports club

All clubs have much the same structure, no matter what size they are or what the sport is.

The job of a sports club is to:
- provide facilities
- organize competitions
- promote the sport
- encourage new members.

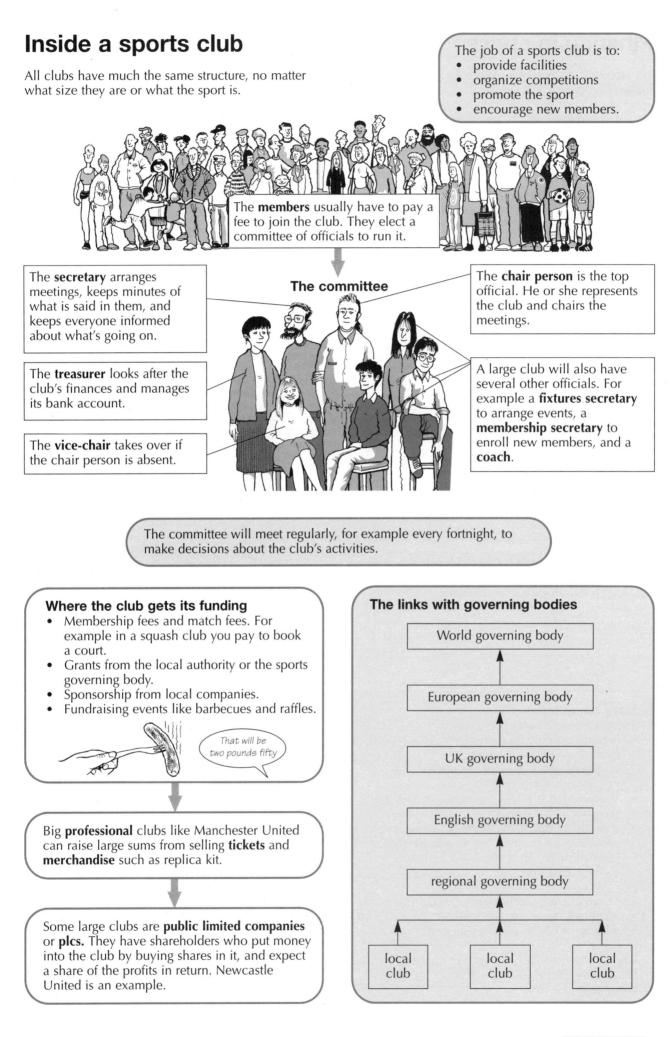

The **members** usually have to pay a fee to join the club. They elect a committee of officials to run it.

**The committee**

The **secretary** arranges meetings, keeps minutes of what is said in them, and keeps everyone informed about what's going on.

The **chair person** is the top official. He or she represents the club and chairs the meetings.

The **treasurer** looks after the club's finances and manages its bank account.

A large club will also have several other officials. For example a **fixtures secretary** to arrange events, a **membership secretary** to enroll new members, and a **coach**.

The **vice-chair** takes over if the chair person is absent.

The committee will meet regularly, for example every fortnight, to make decisions about the club's activities.

## Where the club gets its funding
- Membership fees and match fees. For example in a squash club you pay to book a court.
- Grants from the local authority or the sports governing body.
- Sponsorship from local companies.
- Fundraising events like barbecues and raffles.

*That will be two pounds fifty*

Big **professional** clubs like Manchester United can raise large sums from selling **tickets** and **merchandise** such as replica kit.

Some large clubs are **public limited companies** or **plcs.** They have shareholders who put money into the club by buying shares in it, and expect a share of the profits in return. Newcastle United is an example.

## The links with governing bodies

World governing body

↑

European governing body

↑

UK governing body

↑

English governing body

↑

regional governing body

↑

| local club | local club | local club |

Q10, page 84

# PE and sport in school

- If you take up an activity at school and enjoy it, you are more likely to continue later.
- So the government, the Sports Council and the governing bodies of sport are all keen to promote sport in school.

**The Sports Council**
To find out about the Sports Council and its links with schools, go to page 63.

## The difference between PE and sport

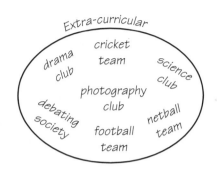
*Extra-curricular*: drama club, cricket team, science club, photography club, debating society, football team, netball team

You study PE in normal lesson time. Everyone from 5 to 16 *must* study it, as part of the National Curriculum approved by the government.

You can take it as an exam subject at GCSE, A level, CFS, and as part of GNVQ courses. So you can improve your skills *and* gain a useful qualification.

But you play **sport** *outside* normal lesson time – lunchtime, evenings or weekends. It is **extra-curricular**, like many school activities.

---

- For GCSE PE, you must study a number of practical activities chosen from the syllabus.
- There are lots to choose from, including games, athletics and dance. What you choose depends on your own interests and abilities, and what the school can offer.

*I personally prefer resting.*

### What activities can a school offer?
It depends on:
- the facilities available. A school may not have the money or space for good sports facilities. Many city schools have no playing fields of their own.
- the expertise available. A school can't offer an activity if there isn't a teacher for it.
- the attitude of the school and the teachers. Sports and other extra-curricular activities depend on teachers giving up free time. Many are happy to do this. But the National Curriculum has led to more work for teachers, and less free time.

---

- You study many health and fitness topics in PE class.
- Some are so important that schools hold **health awareness** days for them, with talks and workshops. For example on smoking, alcohol, drug abuse and AIDS.

### If there's a shortage of resources
If a school is short of facilities or expertise, it can ...
- use the local sports centre, as most schools do for swimming.
- send students off on residential courses for things like sailing and climbing.
- link up with a local sports club, and use the club's facilities and coaching.

---

### Schools and governing bodies
The **governing body** of a sport controls and directs it. For example the Amateur Swimming Association (ASA).

Many governing bodies employ **sports development officers** to work with schools and get students interested in the sport.

Many also run award schemes for young people, to encourage them to participate. For example, the Kellogs/ASA award scheme for swimming, and the Kwik-Cricket award scheme for cricket.

### Links with local clubs
These benefit both the school and the club.
- Students get the chance to play a sport they can't play at school.
- Clubs can provide qualified coaching. Some local clubs send their coaches into schools to help.
- The students may join the club when they leave school. Clubs may encourage this by charging them less to join.

Q11, page 85

# Attitude to sport in different countries

*All governments are interested in sport. Some promote sport for everyone. Some concentrate on the best athletes. Some do both. These are some of the reasons.*

| Why promote sport for all? | Why promote the best athletes? |
|---|---|
| • To keep the nation healthy. Regular exercise means better health and a lower health care bill. | • To give the nation something to be proud of. When athletes win gold everyone feels proud of them. |
| • To cut crime and vandalism. Sport is an outlet for energy. | • To improve the nation's standing in the world. |
| • To unite different cultural groups in the nation. Sport can be shared by everyone. | • To prove that the nation is superior to other nations. |

## In the UK

- The government promotes both sport for all, and excellence in sport, through the Sports Council, and by making PE compulsory in schools.
- But it does not put much money into sport, or fund athletes directly.
- A promising young football player may be spotted by a talent scout and given a club apprenticeship. He may then get a contract as a professional player.
- But for many sports, you have to find a job and a coach, and pay for your training.
- Some sports have 'amateur' status. So you can't earn prize money. (See page 71.)
- Some young athletes do manage to get grants or scholarships or sponsors. But most have to rely on themselves and their families for money.

## In the USA

- PE is not compulsory beyond 14 in most American **high schools** (secondary schools).
- Like the UK, the states promote sport but do not fund athletes directly.
- But unlike the UK, young athletes receive a lot of support from the university or **college** system, which offers grants to athletic students (about $400 million a year).
- You need certain grades to win a grant. But a college really wants your sports skills, because there is fierce competition in sport between colleges.
- A top college team can sell broadcast rights, use of its logo, tickets at the gate and so on.
- Many colleges provide Olympic-level coaching.
- College athletes may go on to play for professional teams. But many leave without even graduating, because they don't study.

## In the developing world

- A third world government can't really promote sport for everyone, because it can't afford to build facilities.
- But top athletes will bring it status. So it is likely to concentrate on sports where it can be successful, and support these athletes directly.
- The top athletes may have 'jobs' where they are given plenty of time to train.
- For example Kenya has produced brilliant middle and long distance runners. Some of them work as PE instructors in the army.

## In former Eastern Bloc countries

- The Eastern Bloc countries included the Soviet Union and East Germany.
- They were **communist**, which means the state controlled everything, including sport.
- The state strongly promoted sport for all, to keep the workers healthy and to strengthen discipline and team work.
- Most factories had sports facilities, with a graded system of exercise for everyone.
- The state also promoted excellence, partly to show that its system was superior.
- It supported its best athletes directly. Young athletes were sent to 'sports schools', often as young as six. Top athletes did not have to work while they trained.
- These countries abandoned communism in the 1980s and 1990s. But they remain strong on sport. China and Cuba are both still communist, and strong on sport.

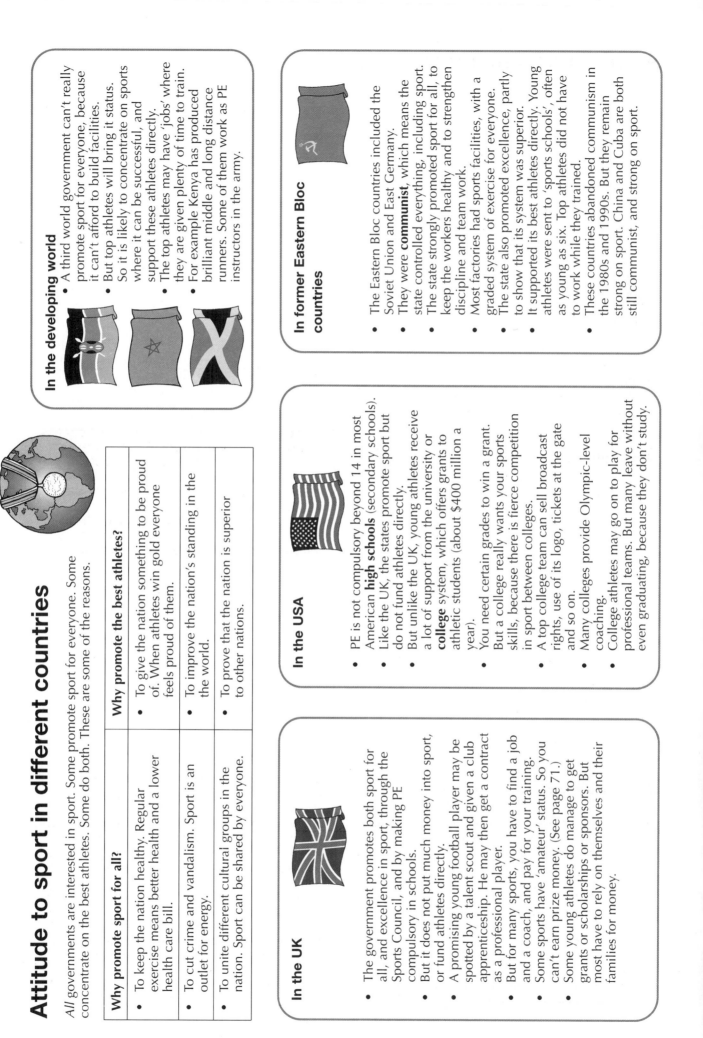

Q12, page 85

# Amateur versus professional

- **Amateurs** don't get paid for playing their sport. Hockey and swimming are amateur sports.
- **Professionals** play full time and get paid for it. It's how they earn their living. Golf, tennis and football can all be played professionally.

## A little history

- The terms **amateur** and **professional** have their origins in the class system.
- **Amateur** meant you were a gentleman who could afford to play sport just for pleasure.
- **Professionals** were lower class people who earned money from sport, often by doing something for a bet.
- In 1866 the Amateur Athletics Club was set up by gentlemen. Working class men were kept out because manual labour made them stronger than the gentlemen.
- In 1880 the club became the Amateur Athletics Association. It changed 'amateur' to mean someone who got no financial reward from a sport. So the working class could now join.

## Amateurism and the Olympic Ideal

- The Olympics were meant for amateurs. Tennis was banned in the 1920s because of doubts about the players' status.
- But since then many competitors have not been true amateurs, and many winners have been rewarded when they got home.
- So in 1981 the term 'Olympic amateur' was dropped from the rules. Tennis was allowed back in 1988.
- The decision about who can take part is now left to the IOC and international governing bodies.
- Some are sticking to the amateur ideal. For example professional boxers still can't take part in the games, while professional footballers can.

## Who decides on status?

- The rules about status are made by the international governing bodies.
- In swimming, hockey and netball, *all* the athletes have amateur status.
- Other sports have amateur and professional levels, with professionals on top. They don't usually compete with each other. Football is an example (except for the FA Cup, where both amateur and professional teams can compete).
- But some sports are **open**, which means amateurs and professionals can compete freely in most events. Horse racing and tennis are examples.

## Are amateurs *really* not paid?

Amateurs can't be paid directly, but there are ways around this. For example:

1  **Scholarships.** In the USA young athletes get sports scholarships to college. There they train with top coaches in top facilities and don't have to worry about money.

2  **Trust funds.** Since 1983, athletes in athletics *can* accept prize and appearance money. But it must be paid into a **trust fund** for them. The fund then pays out money to cover their training and living expenses. The athlete gets the rest on retirement.

3  **'Jobs'.** Athletes may be given token 'jobs', for example as PE instructors in the army, so that they can train full time while being paid. This often happens in developing countries.

## Rugby League and Rugby Union

Rugby League was born in 1895, when 22 northern clubs broke away from Rugby Union. They wanted pay for playing, to make up for the wages they lost when away from work.

Rugby League became the professional game and developed its own rules. Rugby Union remained amateur. Then, in recent years:

- TV started paying very large sums to both sports, for the right to broadcast events.
- This led to very large salaries for Rugby League players – but not for Rugby Union players, who felt badly treated.
- Rugby Union players did however get 'gifts' of things like cars, which in fact broke the amateur rules. (This happens in other sports too!)
- So in 1995, Rugby Union backed down under increasing pressure, and allowed its teams to turn professional.

Q13, page 85

# Sponsorship

**Sponsorship** is where a business provides support for an event or team or individual. The business gets publicity in exchange. Its name or logo is displayed on kit, hoardings and programmes.

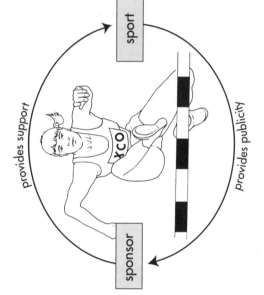

provides support

sport

sponsor

provides publicity

### Examples of sponsorship
- Flora sponsors the London Marathon.
- Sharp sponsors Manchester United.
- her local butcher sponsors Phyllis Smith, British Olympic 400m runner.

### Forms of sponsorship
It may take many forms. For example:
- money. This is the most usual form.
- free flights provided by an airline.
- free food from a supermarket for athletes in training.
- provision of a school playing field.
- a scholarship to an American college or to a training course.

### Advantages to the sponsor
- A link with sport is good for a company's image.
- Sponsorship is often **tax-deductible**. A company won't have to pay tax on the money it gives.
- In a TV sports event, the sponsor's name or logo is seen in millions of homes.
- The sponsor may get the best seats at an event, or the use of luxury executive boxes, and can use these to entertain clients.

### Disadvantages to the sponsor
The sponsor is taking a risk.
- The athlete or team may behave badly, or the event may be disrupted by hooliganism.
- The athlete or team may be so unsuccessful that the sponsor feels it was money down the drain.

### Finding a sponsor
It is difficult, and especially for:
- unknown young athletes. Sponsors like a safe bet!
- a sport that does not have a slot on TV. Big sponsors prefer high-profile TV sports.
- female or black athletes. For example companies who make upmarket cars will choose sports and athletes that most of their customers can identify with – and most of their customers are white males.

### Product endorsement and advertising
- If you're a top athlete, companies will *rush* to pay you to **endorse** their products. For example to wear their clothing, drink their soft drinks and appear in their ads.
- Top athletes can earn more from these deals than from their sport.
- It is not quite the same as sponsorship, since the athletes don't usually need the money to survive!

### Helping the athlete
Sponsorship helps an athlete to cope with expenses like these ...
- coaching fees
- travel to training facilities (which may be overseas)
- use of training facilities
- travel to events
- accommodation away from home
- food, including special diets
- kit and equipment
- physiotherapy.

### Benefits for sport
- Sponsorship makes it possible to run events that would otherwise be too expensive.
- It helps talented athletes to train and compete when they couldn't afford to otherwise.

### Drawbacks for sport
- A sponsorship deal lasts only a certain time. It does not give a team or an athlete long-term security.
- A sponsor may have an unhealthy image. Sponsorship by alcohol and tobacco companies is not allowed for events for the under-18s.
- Sponsors may want to dictate changes that suit them rather than the athletes. For example change the timing of an event to coincide with peak viewing time on TV.

Q14, page 85

# Sport and the media in general

The **media** are all the means by which information is delivered: books, newspapers, magazines, radio, TV, film, video and the Internet.

## How the media affect sport

### +

Media coverage promotes sport. People learn about a sport and may want to try it out.

The media help to educate and inform sports fans, which is healthy for sport.

TV programmes, videos and books can help you learn and improve your sports skills.

The media create sports 'stars' who inspire young athletes and act as role models for them.

A sport with lots of media coverage (especially TV) finds it easier to get sponsorship.

### –

The media puts extra pressure on managers and captains to get results. They may be hounded out of their jobs if they fail.

Sports stars lose privacy. Their private lives get reported on.

A sport may get too much exposure. Many people think this is happening to football.

The media may sensationalize sports news and events to attract more viewers or readers.

Sports that get little or no media attention find it very difficult to get sponsorship.

> The media have the same kinds of effect on dance and other activities.

## How the media present sport

The people who work in the media control what you see, hear and read about sport. For example TV producers, interviewers, newspaper editors and sports reporters. They decide what to put in and what to leave out, depending on whether they want to:
- educate you
- inform you of the facts
- entertain you
- be deliberately sensational
- please sponsors
- express a particular point of view, such as strong disapproval.

## Newspapers
- Sport helps sell newspapers.
- It also helps sell advertising space in them. Some companies prefer to advertise in the sports pages.
- The UK has two types of newspaper, and they tend to treat sport differently.
- The tabloids (like The Daily Mirror and The Sun) go for sensational headlines, take a strong line of approval or disapproval, and do very little on minority sports.
- The broadsheets or quality press (like The Daily Telegraph and The Guardian) go for more thoughtful comment and analysis, and pay more attention to minority sports.

## Magazines
- A good way to find out about the latest developments in your sport.
- Useful when you are buying sports equipment. (They often do test reports.)

## Videos
You can replay them as much as you want. So they're a good way to learn about sports skills.

Q15, page 85

# More about sport and TV

Of all the media, TV has the biggest impact on sport – and vice versa!

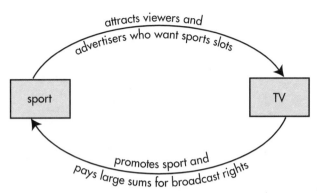

attracts viewers and advertisers who want sports slots

sport

TV

promotes sport and pays large sums for broadcast rights

## TV and the professional athlete

TV has played a big part in the rise of the highly-paid professional athlete.

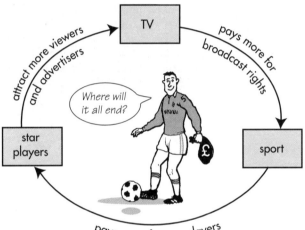

attract more viewers and advertisers

TV

pays more for broadcast rights

Where will it all end?

star players

sport

pays more for star players

- Sport pays big transfer fees and offers big cash prizes to attract 'star' players.
- These players attract more spectators, TV viewers and sponsors.
- This in turn makes more money for sport.
- So sport pays bigger transfer fees and offers bigger cash prizes ... and so on.

## Negative effects of TV

TV has two negative effects on sport that other media don't have.

- When people can watch sport in their homes in comfort, attendance at live events falls.
- It is powerful enough to force changes on a sport. The tie break was brought into tennis to appeal to TV viewers. In 1996 Rugby League stopped being a winter-only game so that TV fans could enjoy it all year round.

## Broadcast rights

- To show a sports event, a TV company must pay for **broadcast rights**. It usually pays the governing body.
- If the company buys **exclusive** rights, only it can film the event.
- It can then sell footage on to other companies and charge a lot. (They might buy just the highlights.)
- Satellite companies are willing to pay *huge* sums for exclusive rights to events like the FA Cup Final.
- But this would be unfair on viewers who don't have satellite dishes.
- So in the 1996 Broadcast Bill, Parliament drew up a list of popular events to which all TV companies must have equal access.

## Some events which can't sell exclusive rights

The Derby
The FIFA world cup finals
The FA Cup Final
The Grand National
The Olympic Games
The finals week of Wimbledon

## Different kinds of TV stations

They are all in competition to show sports events.

| Type | Example(s) | How it transmits | How you pay |
|------|-----------|------------------|-------------|
| Terrestrial | BBC 1 and 2, ITV, Channels 4 and 5 | from a TV mast to your aerial | buy a TV licence |
| Satellite | BSkyB | to your satellite dish via a satellite | take out a subscription |
| Cable | Videotron | via cables below the street with a line into your home | take out a subscription |

- The number of channels offered by satellite and cable companies is growing fast.
- By the end of the decade there will be hundreds of channels, many specializing in sport. Some will be pay-as-you-view.
- It means minority sports will get more coverage. But the 'big' sports may suffer over-exposure, and viewers may get bored.

I think I'll just go and mow the lawn.

Q16, page 85

# Women in physical recreation and sport

## Women in sport

Women's participation in serious sport lags a long way behind men's. These are some reasons.

- **Mistaken beliefs.** It was wrongly thought that many sports could harm women. For example the triple jump – its impact on the lower body would leave them unable to have children.
- **Society's attitudes.** Successful athletes are tough, determined, competitive and very fit. Many men *and* women feel this is 'unfeminine'.
- **Shortage of role models.** In the past there weren't many women to lead the way in UK sport. But this is changing with people like Sally Gunnell and Judy Simpson.
- **The media.** Women's sports don't get much media attention. More attention would lead to more interest.
- **Lack of sponsorship.** Sponsors use sport to sell their products. They go for the sports with most viewers – men's sports. Women's sports have difficulty finding sponsorship – and that means financial problems.

## Women in other areas of sport

- Sport also needs administrators, coaches and teachers.
- These jobs are almost all taken by men, even in women's sports.
- Men control sport at every level from the top down.
- But women are perfectly able for these jobs. The best way to develop women's sports is for women to take responsibility for them.

## The Women's Sports Foundation

This was set up in 1984. It is run by women. Its aims are:
- to help women become involved in sport at all levels and in all areas, including coaching and managing.
- to challenge inequality in sport and bring about change.
- to improve the media coverage of women's sports.

The Foundation works closely with the Sports Council, the CCPR and other organizations, to promote women's sport.

## Women and physical recreation

Women participate less than men in physical recreation. These are some of the reasons.

- **Traditional attitudes.** A woman's place is at home, looking after the family – not out getting sweaty in public. Such attitudes persist among some age groups and cultures.
- **Lack of time and energy.** Bringing up children is hard work. Many women work outside the home *and* bring up children, and feel worn out.
- **Lack of money.** Women who don't have a paid job often don't have money to spend. Baby sitters are an added expense.
- **Problems getting to facilities.** For a woman at home with small children but no car, getting to a facility can take enormous effort. Many women are also afraid to go out alone at night.

Women's participation *is* increasing, especially in activities like aerobics and yoga. Many local authorities encourage participation by running women-only sessions at swimming pools and gyms.

| % participating in physical activity in previous 4 weeks | | |
|---|---|---|
| Year | Male | Female |
| 1987 | 70 | 52 |
| 1990 | 73 | 57 |
| 1993 | 72 | 57 |

Q17, page 85

# Behaviour of players and spectators

## Players

### Sports etiquette

Sports have **rules**. They also have **etiquette**, which is an unwritten code of behaviour. For example:

- a cricket player walks away from the crease as soon as he sees he's out. He doesn't wait to be told.
- when a football player is injured, the ball may be kicked out of play on purpose, to let the player get treatment. When play resumes, it is given back to the team who kicked it out.

### Violence among players

- In sports where there is no physical contact, like swimming and gymnastics, violence among competitors is rare.
- But in sports with a lot of physical contact, like rugby and football, it is quite common.
- It is usually punished by the club or governing body with a fine or suspension. For more serious incidents, the police are called.
- Some people think violence among players encourages violence among spectators and vice versa, but this has not been proved.

## Spectators

### The role of spectators

Spectators and players depend on each other.

emotional and financial support

players

spectators

excitement and enjoyment

- Spectators help their teams by cheering them on. This increases the players' level of **arousal** (page 45).
- They also support them financially when they buy tickets and club merchandise.
- In return, the players provide excitement and enjoyment for spectators.

### Hooliganism

**Football hooligans** are spectators who behave badly at football matches. They throw stones, bottles and other weapons at the opposing fans or onto the pitch. They run riot in streets and pubs around venues.

Hooliganism is often linked with right-wing racist groups. Between the early 1960s and 1990s, hooligans gave English football a bad name all over the world.

'ello!
'ello! 'ello!

### The role of the police

- The police play a big part in controlling crowds at sports events.
- They patrol venues, the streets around them, and local railway stations.
- Clubs have to pay towards police costs.

## Two football tragedies

**Heysel.** In 1985, during the European Cup Final at the Heysel Stadium in Brussels, Liverpool fans rushed at Juventus fans. A wall collapsed killing 39 Juventus fans. English clubs were banned from European competitions for the next 5 years.

**Hillsborough.** In 1989, at the FA Cup semi-final at Hillsborough (Sheffield), a large crowd of Liverpool fans were still outside the ground before kick-off. The police opened a large gate to let them in. In the rush for the terraces, fans were trapped against the perimeter fence. 99 fans were crushed to death.

## The Taylor report

Hillsborough led to an enquiry and the **Taylor Report**. This said that perimeter fences should be removed and stadiums made all-seater, with no more standing on terraces. Clubs were forced to spend thousands of pounds making their stadiums safer. The Football Association helped out with grants.

## Controlling crowd behaviour

Hooliganism and the Hillsborough tragedy led to these steps for controlling football crowds:

- fences at stadiums to keep rival fans apart.
- closed circuit TV cameras around stadiums.
- club membership schemes to make it easier to bar troublemakers.
- a ban by some clubs on all away fans.
- police in different cities and countries sharing information about hooligans.
- perimeter fences removed.
- no more standing on the terraces.

Q18, page 85

# International sport

- Most sports hold international events. These are arranged by their international governing bodies.
- The Commonwealth Games and the Olympics cover a range of sports. They are arranged by special committees with help from governing bodies. (The International Olympics Committee arranges the Olympics.)

> **Example: football**
> - The European Nations Championship is arranged by UEFA (the European governing body).
> - The World Cup is arranged by FIFA (the World governing body).

## The benefits of international sport

*sport not war*

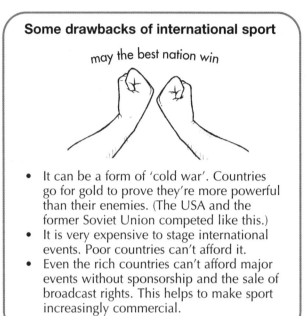

- It gives players and supporters from different countries the chance to meet and develop friendships.
- It unites people of different race, culture and religion in a shared interest.
- It gives the world's top athletes the chance to compete against each other. This encourages excellence.
- It spreads interest in sport around the world and encourages more people to play.

## Some drawbacks of international sport

*may the best nation win*

- It can be a form of 'cold war'. Countries go for gold to prove they're more powerful than their enemies. (The USA and the former Soviet Union competed like this.)
- It is very expensive to stage international events. Poor countries can't afford it.
- Even the rich countries can't afford major events without sponsorship and the sale of broadcast rights. This helps to make sport increasingly commercial.

## Hosting international events
- The **host** is the city or country staging the events. The **venue** is the stadium where an event is held.
- The Olympics are hosted by cities. Events like the European Nations Championships for football are hosted by a country and spread around different venues.

> *honey, I'm home*
>
> England hosted the European Nations Championship in 1996, with venues in 8 cities including Leeds, Sheffield and London.

## Advantages and disadvantages of playing host

### +

Brings **prestige.** A successful event pays off later in all kinds of ways. For example extra trade and tourism.

Boosts **facilities.** Cities build or improve sport, transport and other facilities to host events. Locals enjoy these long after the events.

May make **profit** for its organizers (from sales of TV rights, tickets and merchandise).

Good for local **business** – shops, restaurants, hotels, taxis and other services.

### –

Brings **security risks**. Terrorists and other groups may use an event to air their grievances. Hooligans from other countries may visit.

May bring huge **losses**, if the host has problems organizing the event.

**Costs** increase as events get more glamorous and security more expensive.

Millions of visitors means extra **strain** on phone systems, transport and so on. If they can't cope it leads to problems and frustration.

Q19, page 85

# Trouble at the games!

The Summer Olympics is the world's biggest and most spectacular sports event.
That means it is also open to big financial, political and racial problems.

## 1936 Berlin
- The games were awarded to Berlin in 1931. By 1936 Hitler and the Nazis were in power.
- Hitler used the games to show off Nazi power and the 'supremacy' of the blonde blue-eyed Northern races.
- But the black American athlete Jesse Owens was the star of the Games, with 4 gold medals. When the crowd rose to salute Owens, Hitler left the stadium.

## 1968 Mexico City
- The homeless were cleared off the streets so that visitors wouldn't see them.
- Students rioted about this and the money 'wasted' on the games. Over 300 students were shot dead by the army.
- Winning black American sprinters Tommie Smith and John Carlos gave a 'black power' salute during their medal ceremony. They were expelled by the US Olympic Association and sent home immediately.

## 1972 Munich
- Palestinian terrorists broke into the Olympic village, took 9 Israeli athletes hostage and killed 2 others. They demanded the release of 200 Palestinians held in Israeli prisons.
- A failed rescue attempt by German police led to the death of the athletes, a policeman and 5 terrorists.

## 1976 Montreal
- The Canadian government made lavish plans for the games. But after a long hard winter of industrial disputes the money ran out.
- The stadium for the opening ceremony was unfinished. Accommodation for the athletes was poor.
- Montreal is *still* paying off its $1 billion Olympic debts.
- African countries asked the IOC to ban New Zealand, because of its rugby links with apartheid South Africa. The IOC refused, and 22 black African teams flew home again.

## 1980 Moscow
- The Soviet Union had invaded Afghanistan in December 1979.
- In protest, West Germany, Kenya, Japan, the USA and Canada boycotted these games.

## 1984 Los Angeles
- These were the first games to be completely funded by sponsorship and the sale of broadcast rights. Profits: $235 million!
- Some people felt they were too commercial and that athletes were being exploited.
- They were boycotted by the Soviet Union and many of its allies. These gave poor security as the reason, but it was really to pay America back for boycotting Moscow.

## 1988 Seoul
- Seoul is in capitalist South Korea. Communist North Korea wanted to host some of the events. The IOC refused, so North Korea and four allies boycotted the games.
- Tennis returned at these games. It had been banned in 1924 because its players were not amateurs. But the rule about amateur status for athletes was dropped in 1981.

## 1992 Barcelona
- No boycotts.
- The trend towards commercialisation continued and the games made a small profit.
- South Africa sent a team for the first time in over 30 years. (It was expelled in the 1960s because of apartheid.)
- East and West Germany combined to form a single team for the first time since 1964.

> **The Olympic ideals**
> - personal excellence
> - sport as education
> - cultural exchange
> - mass participation
> - fair play
> - international understanding
>
> As you can see from this page, the games can't always live up to these ideals!

Q20, page 85

# The question bank

- These exam-level questions will help you revise.
- The number in the grey arrow shows which revision page they refer to.
- Try answering them without looking back at the revision page.
- You can check your answers in the Answer section which starts on page 86.

## Part one: The body

**p4**   **1**   Fitness is the ability to meet the demands of the environment.
(a) Explain what this means, using a building worker as example.
(b) Why might an elderly person want to exercise?

**p5**   **2**   Figure 1 shows two body systems.

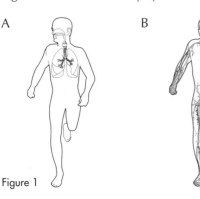

A       B

Figure 1

(a) Name the two body systems.
(b) State the **main organ** in each system.
(c) For each system describe **two** changes that take place during vigorous exercise.
(d) Name **two** other body systems.

**p6**   **3**   The **clavicle** is:
A. a valve in the heart.
B. a bone in the lower leg.
C. a bone below the neck.
D. a muscle attached to the cranium.
Select the correct letter.

**p6**   **4**   (a) Write down **two** functions of the skeleton.
(b) Name **two** organs protected by the ribs.
(c) Name **one** organ protected by the cranium.

**p7**   **5**   Figure 2 shows a long bone.

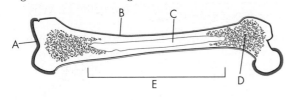

Figure 2

(a) Name the parts labelled A, B, C, D and E.

(b) **Red cells** are formed in some bones. Where in the bone does this take place?
(c) What is the function of **calcium** in bones?
(d) Name **two** long bones in the lower leg.
(e) Explain why strong bones are important for a gymnast.

**6**   (a) Explain what a **joint** is, in the human body.   **p8**
(b) Give **one** example of:
(i) a slightly movable joint;
(ii) a fixed joint.
(c) Without synovial joints, you could not run. Explain.

**7**   Figure 3 shows a joint in the body.   **p9**

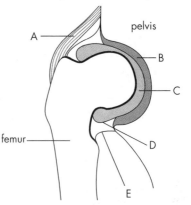

Figure 3

(a) Name the parts labelled A, B, C, D, E, and F.
(b) (i) Which type of joint is this?
(ii) Where is it in the body?
(iii) Name another joint of this type.
(c) Apart from rotation, state **two** other types of motion that take place at this joint.
(d) Name an **injury** that often occurs in old people at this joint, when they fall.

**8**   (a) Name the muscles at A and B in Figure 4.   **p10**

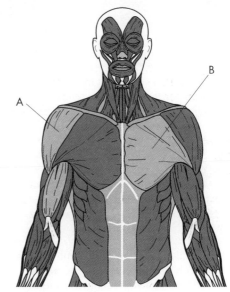

Figure 4

(b) Say whether they are voluntary or involuntary and explain your answer.
(c) Explain the function of each muscle.

p11 **9** Figure 5 shows an arm bending at the elbow.

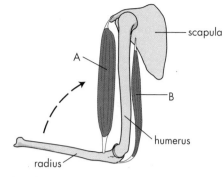

Figure 5

(a) Name the muscles labelled A and B.
(b) Where is the **origin** of A?
(c) When the arm bends at the elbow, which muscle acts as the **agonist**? Explain.
(d) Explain how A and B work together to make the elbow bend.
(e) Explain how A and B will work together to straighten the elbow again.

p12 **10** Figure 6 shows a simple plan of the **circulatory system**.

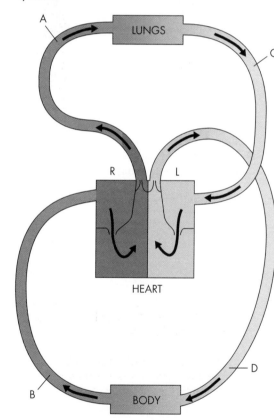

Figure 6

(a) (i) Which **two** letters represent arteries?
    (ii) Which letter represents the **aorta**?
(b) (i) Which letter represents the **pulmonary vein**?
    (ii) Explain how this vein is different from other veins.
(c) Name two **disorders** of the circulatory system.

**11** In Figure 7, A, B, C and D are the four chambers of the heart. p12

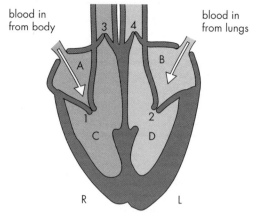

Figure 7

(a) What is the heart made of?
(b) 1, 2, 3 and 4 are valves. What is their function?
(c) (i) What happens when A and B contract?
    (ii) What happens when C and D contract?
(d) D has the thickest walls. Explain why.
(e) (i) What are A and B called?
    (ii) What are C and D called?
(f) Name **two** valves of the heart.

**12** (a) What is the function of **haemoglobin** in red blood cells? p13
(b) Name a **mineral** needed to make haemoglobin.
(c) (i) Name **one** nutrient carried in blood plasma.
    (ii) Name **one** waste substance carried in blood plasma.

**13** All these help oxygen to reach the muscles: p14
A. bronchi;
B. alveoli;
C. blood;
D. trachea;
E. capillary walls;
F. nose;
G. bronchioles.
Arrange the letters A – G in order, to show the path of oxygen from the air to the muscles.

**14** (a) Describe the changes that take place in the chest to draw air into the lungs, when you breathe in. p15
(b) (i) What is **vital capacity**?
    (ii) Does it change as you get fitter? Explain why.
(c) The air you breathe out contains more water vapour than the air you breathe in. Why?

**15** In the body, energy is obtained from glucose. p16
(a) Which body system breaks down food?
(b) (i) Which nutrient in food breaks down to glucose?
    (ii) Name **two** foods that contain this nutrient.
(c) In what form is glucose stored in muscles?
(d) Where else in the body is glucose stored in this form?

p17
**16** (a) Muscles obtain energy from glucose in a process called **aerobic respiration**.
  (i) What other substance is needed for this?
  (ii) Name the two waste substances produced and describe how they are excreted.
 (b) During very strenuous exercise, energy is produced **without** using oxygen.
  (i) What is this process called?
  (ii) The body can endure very strenuous exercise for only a short time. Explain why.
 (c) Why does the body get warmer during exercise?

p18
**17** These are two of the changes that take place in Sam's body, during a training run.
 (a) His heart beats faster.
 (b) He breathes more heavily.
 Explain how each change is helpful to Sam.

p19
**18** When you exercise, your body loses heat by evaporation and radiation.
 (a) Explain how these processes take place.
 (b) State **two** things to do after an exercise session, connected with evaporation.

p20
**19** Figure 8 shows how Sam's heart rate changed during a run on a flat track.

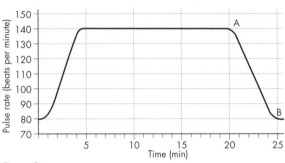

Figure 8

 (a) What was his resting heart rate?
 (b) What was the maximum heart rate reached?
 (c) (i) What was happening between A and B?
  (ii) Name one other change that took place in Sam's body, between A and B.
 (d) How would the graph change if Sam were fitter?

p21
**20** Figure 9 shows three body types, A, B and C.

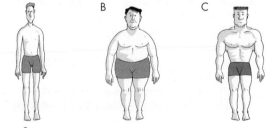

Figure 9

 (a) Name each body type.
 (b) Which suits distance running best? Why?
 (c) **Ecto-mesomorph** means mainly mesomorph but with some ectomorph characteristics. This body type suits basketball. Why?
 (d) (i) Describe an **endo-mesomorph** body type.
  (ii) Explain why it suits shot putt.

## Part two: Getting and staying fit

**1** Components of **health-related fitness** include: p22
 A. flexibility, stamina, and good co-ordination.
 B. muscular endurance, muscular power, and fast reactions.
 C. agility, good co-ordination, and good balance.
 D. flexibility, speed, and body composition.
 Select the correct letter.

**2** For A, B and C in Figure 1, say which component of skills-related fitness is needed. p22

Figure 1

**3** (a) Describe **two** changes that take place in the body with age, which may reduce a person's fitness. p23
 (b) Males tend to be bigger and stronger than females. Why?
 (c) Explain how high altitude can affect fitness for a distance runner.

**4** (a) Write down another name for aerobic fitness. p24
 (b) Name **two** tests for aerobic fitness.
 (c) Liz and Molly go for a run. Liz is aerobically fit, but Molly is not. How will this become obvious during the run?

**5** (a) What is tested in the **sit-and-reach** test? p25
 (b) In a fitness test, Sarah does as many sit-ups as possible in three minutes. What is being tested?

**6** Explain the principle of **progression** in training. p26

**7** (a) (i) What does **hypertrophy** mean? p26
  (ii) Suggest a way to achieve hypertrophy.
 (b) Write down a word that means the opposite.

**8** (a) In planning a training programme for a footballer, name **two** aspects of skills-related fitness you would aim to improve. p27
 (b) For one of these, suggest **one** exercise that will lead to improvement.

p28
**9** Your **heart rate** is a good indication of how hard you work during exercise.
(a) What is the maximum heart rate for a 16-year-old?
(b) Explain the term **aerobic training threshold**.
(c) Say whether this threshold rises, or falls, as you get fitter.
(d) Give **two** activities used to train the cardio-respiratory (aerobic) system.

p29
**10** This is what Jo does during a training session:
Sprints for 30 metres.
Then jogs for 1 minute.
Repeats this pattern eight times.
Rests for 5 minutes.
Repeats the whole thing three times.
(a) What training method is Jo using?
(b) How many **sets** does Jo do?
(c) How many **reps** does she do in a set?
(d) Write down **one** advantage and **one** disadvantage of this training method.

p30
**11** (a) Weight training is used to improve both **strength** and **endurance** of muscles. Say how:
(i) the size of the weights
(ii) the number of reps
will differ for these two purposes.
(b) (i) How would you use weights to improve explosive strength?
(ii) Name **two** sports in which explosive strength is an advantage.

p31
**12** Figure 2 shows two muscle exercises.

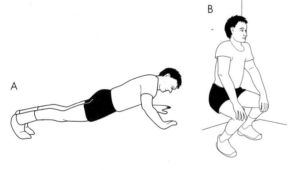

Figure 2

(a) What is an **isometric** muscle contraction?
(b) Which exercise above is isometric?
(c) State **one** advantage and **one** disadvantage of isometric exercises.
(d) (i) Name the type of muscle contraction that takes place in the other exercise.
(ii) Identify **one** other exercise that uses this type of contraction.

p32
**13** (a) What is **circuit training**?
(b) Name **two** activities you could include in a circuit to improve muscular endurance.
(c) Give **two** advantages of circuit training.

p33
**14** (a) (i) Which component of fitness is improved by **stretching**?
(ii) Is this component health-related, or skills-related?

(b) Give **one** example of how this component of fitness helps an athlete.
(c) Explain the difference between **active** and **passive** stretching.

p34
**15** Every training session should include a **warm up** and a **cool down**.
(a) List the benefits of doing a warm up.
(b) Give one benefit of **stretching** as part of the **cool down**.

p35
**16** Figure 3 shows the stages in an athlete's year.

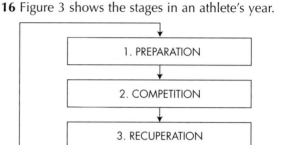

Figure 3

(a) Name two risks the athlete runs during the competition season, which would damage the athlete's performance.
(b) How is the recuperation period likely to affect a chronic knee injury?
(c) In what circumstances might an athlete need to go abroad for training, and how might this affect the athlete?

p36
**17** Describe the effects of regular aerobic cycling sessions on each labelled part of the body, in Figure 4.

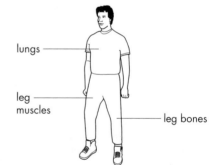

Figure 4

p37
**18** (a) Which nutrient helps to repair muscle damage?
(b) Give the main nutrient for providing energy for exercise.
(c) Explain why fibre is not a nutrient.
(d) Why is vitamin D important for athletes?

p38
**19** (a) What is a **balanced diet**?
(b) What should be the main component of a balanced diet?
(c) 'Keeping weight under control means getting the energy balance right.' Explain.

p39
**20** Name and describe one condition that may result if a diet is not balanced.

## Part three: Learning and playing a sport

**p40** **1** (a) Some skills are performed in a continually changing environment.
   (i) What are these skills called?
   (ii) Give **one** example.
   (iii) For your example in (ii), explain what the environment is, and how it changes.
   (b) Explain the difference between a **skill** and a **performance**.

**p41** **2** Figure 1 shows the information processing system.

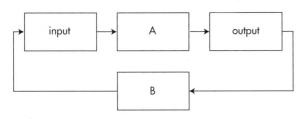

Figure 1

   (a) What do A and B represent?
   (b) Explain what **input** is and give **one** example from any sport other than tennis.
   (c) In which part of the information processing system does coaching play an important role?
   (d) Explain the role of **memory** in the performance of a skill.

**p42** **3** When learning a **complex** skill, it is best to break it into parts and practice each part separately.
   (a) Explain why, using the idea of limited channel capacity.
   (b) What is this type of practice called?
   (c) Name **one** skill you could practice this way.
   (d) Name **one** type of **guidance** that would be appropriate for the skill you chose in (c).

**p43** **4** There are two types of **feedback** in sport.
   (a) Name them and give **one** example of each.
   (b) Give **two** reasons why feedback is important in learning a new skill.

**p44** **5** (a) Name **two** psychological (mental) factors that affect sports performance.
   (b) Diet also affects sports performance. Explain, with examples.

**p45** **6** Figure 2 shows how the quality of performance changes with arousal.

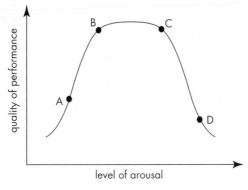

Figure 2

   (a) Explain what **arousal** means, for a sports performance.
   (b) Describe **two** physical symptoms that indicate a high level of arousal.
   (c) At A on the graph, is the athlete over-aroused or under-aroused? What effect will this have on performance?
   (d) Between which points on the graph will the athlete perform best?
   (e) Describe **two** methods of increasing arousal from A to B.

**7** (a) Define **motivation**.  **p46**
   (b) Give **one** example of an extrinsic motivator in tennis.
   (c) In training for a sport, having a goal to aim for can be a good motivator. Explain why the goal should be:
   (i) realistic;
   (ii) exciting.
   (d) 'I must swim a length faster at my next attempt.' Is this a suitable goal? Explain why.

**8** In sport, aggression may be defined as acting  **p47** forcefully within the rules, in order to achieve your aim.
   (a) In which of these sports is aggression most obvious? Explain your choice.
   (i) Golf.
   (ii) Rugby.
   (iii) Mountaineering.
   (b) Aggression in gymnastics is not obvious. Explain how a gymnast might show aggressive behaviour in her sport.
   (c) Choose a sport you are familiar with (not gymnastics) and give **one** example of aggressive behaviour within the rules.

**9** (a) Write down **two** characteristics of an  **p48** extrovert, in terms of sport.
   (b) From the sports below, choose **two** you would expect an introvert to enjoy.
   Tennis
   Rugby
   Fishing
   Hill walking
   Netball

**10** (a) Describe **two** ways in which smoking  **p49** reduces the amount of oxygen reaching muscles.
   (b) How would this affect an athlete?

**11** (a) One class of drug that is banned by the IOC  **p50** promotes muscle growth. What is it called?
   (b) Give **one** example of a sport where athletes might be tempted to use this type of drug.
   (c) Give **two** negative effects of this type of drug on the body.

**12** **Athlete's foot** is a foot infection.  **p51**
   (a) What are the symptoms?
   (b) Give **two** things you can do to avoid it.
   (c) How should it be treated?
   (d) Name **one** other foot infection which can be picked up in the same environment.

p52
**13** (a) Describe **three** things a player can do before a game, to reduce the risk of injury.
(b) Many of the rules of sport are designed to promote safe play. Give two examples.
(c) (i) Define **chronic injury**.
(ii) Write down **one** cause of chronic injury.
(iii) Name a chronic injury associated with golf.

p53
**14** Joint injuries include:
A. fractures, pulls, and dislocations.
B. torn cartilage, dislocations, and sprains.
C. strains, sprains, and bruises.
D. torn cartilage, swelling, and strains.
Select the correct letter.

p53
**15** (a) What signs would you look for, to confirm that an injury was a fracture?
(b) State one thing you must **not** do when dealing with a fracture.

p54
**16** (a) What is a **strain**?
(b) Describe **two** things you could do to relieve the pain from a minor strain in a leg muscle.

p55
**17** (a) In treating sports injuries, what do the letters RICE stand for?
(b) What is the purpose of elevation?
(c) How would you apply compression, during RICE?
(d) Name one injury you would treat using RICE.
(e) Explain why **swelling** and **bruising** usually accompany injury to bones and joints.

p56
**18** (a) What do the letters DRABC stand for?
(b) How can you tell that a person is unconscious?
(c) Why is it important to clear the airway, in an unconscious person?
(d) When someone collapses, you should rush immediately to help them. Do you agree? Explain.

p57
**19** The instructions for **mouth-to-mouth ventilation** are jumbled up below. Write the letters A – F in the correct order.
A. Seal your lips around the casualty's open mouth.
B. Repeat with 1 breath every 6 seconds.
C. Pinch the casualty's nostrils closed.
D. Take your mouth away and breathe in.
E. Tilt the casualty's chin up, and the head back.
F. Breathe out smoothly and firmly into the casualty's mouth.

p58
**20** During a match, a player suffers a sharp blow to the head.
(a) What condition could this lead to?
(b) Give **two** symptoms of this condition.

## Part four: Sport in society

**1** Define **leisure** and explain the growth in it. p59

**2** Give **three** benefits to a school leaver of joining a health club. p60

**3** The elderly tend to choose different physical activities than young people do. Explain why, and give examples. p61

**4** Below are three different groups of users who may visit a sports centre. For each group, state two provisions or facilities that would encourage regular use. p62
(a) Mothers and toddlers.
(b) The disabled.
(c) Young school leavers.

**5** The Sports Council is an organization concerned with sport. p63
(a) Describe the structure of the Sports Council.
(b) State its aims.
(c) Identify two ways in which it encourages sport in schools.

**6** (a) Figure **1** shows the logo of an organization. p64

Figure 1

(i) What do the letters stand for?
(ii) Describe two ways in which this organization benefits its members.
(b) Choose **two** of these national governing bodies of sport and write down their full names.
LTA    FA    ASA    AAA    EBBA
(c) Give three functions of a national governing body.

**7** Say what the initials stand for and give **one** function of the organization. p65
(a) IOC
(b) SAF

**8** (a) What is the main purpose of the National Coaching Foundation? p66
(b) The proposed National Academy of Sport may be one large centre, or several smaller centres in different places. What are the advantages and disadvantages of having one large centre?

**9** (a) (i) Explain how money from the National Lottery reaches sport. p67
(ii) Television companies pay large sums of money to sport. Why?
(b) Give two ways this money is used in sport.

**10** (a) What is the function of the treasurer, in a sports club? p68
(b) Describe **three** ways in which a small local sports club could raise money.

p69 **11** (a) Explain the difference between **PE** and **sport** in school.

(b) Some schools form strong links with **sports clubs**. State the benefits of this arrangement.

p70 **12** (a) Promising young athletes are treated quite differently in the UK and China. Briefly describe the main differences.

(b) State how a sports scholarship to an American college would benefit a young British athlete.

p71 **13** (a) Explain the difference between **amateurs** and **professionals** in sport.

(b) Define an **open** event in sport.

(c) Some activities which were once 'amateur only' have now become 'open'. Give **one** advantage and **one** disadvantage of this change.

p72 **14** The athlete in Figure 2 is sponsored by a company called XCO.

Figure 2

(a) State **two** forms this sponsorship could take.

(b) How does it benefit XCO?

(c) Give **two** arguments in favour of banning sports sponsorship by cigarette companies.

p73 **15** 'Watching a sports event on TV is better than being there.' Discuss this statement.

p74 **16** In sports like golf and tennis, top players can earn a great deal of money. Explain how TV has helped to bring about this situation.

p75 **17** The **Women's Sports Foundation** aims to improve media coverage of women's sports. How will this benefit women's sports?

p76 **18** (a) Explain how **spectators** and **players** depend on each other, in sports like football.

(b) How might the behaviour of spectators affect an athlete's performance? Give examples.

(c) How has the Taylor Report affected sports venues in this country?

p77 **19** (a) Cities around the world compete fiercely for the chance to host the Summer Olympics. Why?

(b) List **three** disadvantages to a country of hosting an international sports event.

p78 **20** Describe problems that have affected **two** Summer Olympics since 1972.

# Answers

## Part one: The body

**1** **(a)** A building worker may have to push and carry heavy loads, and bend and stretch repeatedly for long periods. He is on his feet all day long. If he is fit he can cope with all this without getting too tired.
**(b)** These are all good reasons: to keep healthy and fit, in order to stay active and enjoy life; to prevent stiffness; to keep weight down; to prevent problems such as heart disease; to reduce stress caused by loneliness; to meet people (for example in an exercise class or at swimming).

**2** **(a)** A: respiratory system. B: circulatory system.
**(b)** In A, the lungs. In B, the heart. **(c)** *For each system, any two of the following answers.*
In A: breathing gets deeper; it also gets faster; more oxygen is taken in with each breath; more carbon dioxide is removed with each breath. In B: the heart beats faster; more blood is pumped with each beat; blood pressure rises; arterioles widen; more blood is shunted to the muscles; blood vessels under the skin dilate in order to cool the blood. **(d)** *Any two of these systems:* skeletal, hormonal, nervous, muscular, digestive, excretory.

**3** C.

**4** **(a)** *Any two of these:* to support the body; to protect internal organs; to allow movement; to make blood cells (in the red marrow found in some bones).
**(b)** the heart and lungs **(c)** the brain

**5** **(a)** A - cartilage; B - the periosteum; C- the marrow cavity; D - spongy bone; E - the diaphysis.
**(b)** In red marrow in spongy bone. **(c)** It is present as calcium salts. These make bone hard and strong by forming a cement in which fibres are embedded.
**(d)** the tibia and fibula **(e)** Because movements in gymnastics can put a lot of stress on the bones. For example an arm and hand may have to support the full weight of the body.

**6** **(a)** A joint is where bones meet. It allows movement.
**(b)** **(i)** The joints between most vertebrae, for example between the lumbar vertebrae. *Or* the joints between the sternum and ribs. **(ii)** the joints between the plates in the cranium, or the fused joints between vertebrae in the sacrum or coccyx.
**(c)** Synovial joints are freely movable joints. For running, you need a good range of movement at the hip, knee, elbow, shoulder and ankle joints. All these joints are synovial.

**7** **(a)** A - ligament; B - cartilage; C - joint cavity; D - synovial membrane; E - joint capsule.
**(b)** **(i)** ball-and-socket **(ii)** at the hip
**(iii)** the shoulder joint **(c)** *Any two of these:* extension, flexion, abduction, adduction, circumduction. **(d)** a dislocated hip.

**8** **(a)** A - deltoids; B - pectorals. **(b)** Voluntary - they work only when you want them to.
**(c)** The deltoids raise your arms forwards, sideways, and backwards at your shoulders. The pectorals raise your arms at the shoulders and draw them across your chest.

**9** **(a)** A - biceps; B - triceps. **(b)** on the scapula
**(c)** the biceps. It is the one that shortens or contracts. **(d)** When the biceps contracts, the radius is pulled towards the shoulder. At the same time the triceps relaxes to let the radius move.

**(e)** The triceps will contract to pull the radius down, at the elbow joint. The biceps will relax to let the radius move.

**10** **(a)** **(i)** A and D **(ii)** D **(b)** **(i)** C **(ii)** It carries oxygenated blood. All the other veins carry deoxygenated blood. **(c)** *Any two of:* hardened arteries, heart attack, high blood pressure, blood clots.

**11** **(a)** cardiac muscle **(b)** to prevent blood flowing backwards **(c)** **(i)** Blood from A is squeezed into C. Blood from B is squeezed into D. **(ii)** Blood from C is pumped to the lungs. Blood from D is pumped around the body. **(d)** It has to pump the blood furthest - all around the body. **(e)** **(i)** the atria (each is an atrium) **(ii)** the ventricles. **(f)** *Any two of:* the bicuspid, the tricuspid, the semilunar valves.

**12** **(a)** It combines with oxygen, so that the blood can carry oxygen to the cells. **(b)** iron **(c)** **(i)** glucose **(ii)** carbon dioxide *or* water, from respiration in cells.

**13** F, D, A, G, B, E, C.

**14** **(a)** The diaphragm contracts and straightens. The intercostal muscles contract, pulling the rib cage upwards and outwards. Both these changes make the chest cavity larger, so the lungs also expand, sucking in air. **(b)** **(i)** It is the maximum volume of air you can breathe out, after breathing in as hard as you can. **(ii)** Yes, it increases. As you get fitter, the diaphragm and intercostal muscles get stronger. So they can contract more strongly, which makes the chest cavity larger. This means the lungs can expand more too, taking in and breathing out more air.
**(c)** Because some of the water vapour produced by respiration in cells is carried to the lungs by your blood, and breathed out.

**15** **(a)** The digestive system. **(b)** **(i)** carbohydrates **(ii)** *Any two of:* rice, pasta, potatoes, bread, bananas, chocolate, biscuits. **(c)** As glycogen. **(d)** In the liver.

**16** **(a)** **(i)** oxygen **(ii)** carbon dioxide, which is breathed out through the lungs; and water, which is breathed out as water vapour and excreted in urine.
**(b)** **(i)** anaerobic respiration **(ii)** Because anaerobic respiration produces lactic acid which causes muscle pain and fatigue. **(c)** A lot of the energy from respiration in muscle fibres is produced in the form of heat. During exercise, respiration in the muscle fibres increases. The blood carries the extra heat around the body, making the body warmer.

**17** **(a)** This means more blood gets pumped to the muscles each minute, bringing oxygen for energy and carrying carbon dioxide away. **(b)** Heavier breathing means he takes in more oxygen with each breath, to provide energy for the working muscles.

**18** **(a)** In evaporation, body heat is used to make sweat evaporate. So the body loses heat - it gets cooler. In radiation, blood flowing under the skin loses heat to the air, just like the hot water flowing through a radiator does.
**(b)** Drink water to make up for the water lost as sweat, and have a shower to remove traces of sweat.

**19** **(a)** 75 bpm **(b)** 140 bpm
**(c)** **(i)** Sam had stopped running so his heart rate fell again - he was recovering. **(ii)** *Any one of these changes:* he sweated less; his breathing slowed down; his skin got less flushed. **(d)** If he were fitter his heart rate would be lower at every point, and would return to normal faster after the run. So the curve would be lower on the y-axis, and slope more steeply on the right. *(Hint: you could sketch the two graphs, for this answer!)*

**20 (a)** A - ectomorph; B - endomorph; C - mesomorph. **(b)** A. A slim body means the distance runner has less weight to carry. He or she needs good aerobic fitness and muscular endurance rather than muscular strength. **(c)** A basketball player needs powerful muscles for jumping and shooting; but it helps to be 'linear', with little or no fat, because that just adds weight. **(d) (i)** A well-muscled body with a fair amount of fat. **(ii)** A shot putter needs powerful muscles for throwing; a heavy body helps him (or her) throw with force and stay balanced during the throw.

## Part two: Getting and staying fit

**1** D

**2** A - agility; B - explosive strength (power); C - balance.

**3 (a)** *Any two of these changes*: muscles weaken; bones get lighter; joints stiffen; movement slows; body fat increases. **(b)** The male hormone testosterone promotes the growth of muscle and bone. **(c)** At high altitude the air is thinner, so you take in less oxygen with each breath. Even if a distance runner gulps air, he or she may not get enough oxygen, so will run more slowly and tire sooner than usual. He or she may feel dizzy and weak. But over time, the athlete will acclimatise - the body will produce more red cells to capture as much oxygen as possible.

**4 (a)** cardiovascular endurance or cardio-respiratory fitness (since it refers to the fitness of the heart / lung team). **(b)** *Any two* of: the cycle ergonometer test; the Harvard step test; the Cooper test; the multistage fitness test. (*Your teacher may also have taught you some others.*) **(c)** Liz will be able to run for longer than Molly without tiring or getting 'puffed out', and her heart will not beat so fast.

**5 (a)** the flexibility of the hip joints **(b)** the endurance of the abdominal muscles. (*When a test goes on for more than 30 - 60 seconds it is testing endurance rather than strength.*)

**6** The body adapts only a little a time (or progressively) to extra stress. This means you should increase your exercise level gradually, in a training programme. Otherwise you run the risk of injury.

**7 (a) (i)** thickening of the muscles **(ii)** weight training using heavy weights **(b)** atrophy

**8 (a)** *The best choice would be any two of these:* power (for kicking the ball and jumping for it), agility (so the footballer can change direction fast), and speed of reaction (for ball control). **(b)** For power, a suitable exercise would be weight training for the leg muscles, using machine weights. For agility, sprints around an obstacle course of plastic cones. For speed of reaction, you could get several team mates to kick or throw balls rapidly to the player at the same time.

**9 (a)** 204 bpm (or 220 - age). **(b)** It is the minimum heart rate you must reach during exercise, in order to gain aerobic benefit. It is generally at least 60% of the maximum possible heart rate, but the exact figure depends on your fitness. **(c)** It rises. **(d)** *They should be rhythmic activities that use large muscles, so any two of these would be fine*: walking; jogging; cycling; swimming; skipping; cross-country skiing; or using an exercise bike, rowing machine or treadmill.

**10 (a)** interval training **(b)** 3 **(c)** 8 **(d)** Advantage: you can mix aerobic and anaerobic work in the same training session. This matches what goes on in many team sports. But it is also good for individual sports such as athletics. Disadvantage: you need a lot of determination to keep going.

**11 (a) (i)** Heavy weights for strength, lighter weights for endurance. **(ii)** Few reps for strength, many reps for endurance. **(b) (i)** Use heavy weights, and move them very fast, with low reps. **(ii)** *Any two of these sports:* shot putt, javelin, tennis, football, squash, basketball, long jump, high jump.

**12 (a)** The muscle contracts but remains the same length. **(b)** Exercise B. **(c)** Advantage - *any one of these:* quick to do; no equipment needed; can do them anywhere; they don't hurt. Disadvantage - *one of these:* a muscle gains strength only at the angle used in the exercise; they can be dangerous for people with heart problems. **(d) (i)** isotonic **(ii)** *Any one of these or similar exercises where movement takes place:* chins; press-ups; sit-ups; dips; dorsal raises; or exercises using machine weights or free weights (except for isokinetic machines).

**13 (a)** In circuit training, exercise areas or stations are arranged in a circuit, and you follow the circuit, doing a different exercise at each station. **(b)** *Any two of these or similar exercises:* press-ups, sit-ups, dips, chins, dorsal raises, step-ups. **(c)** *Any two of these advantages:* it is adaptable - you can design it to suit any particular purpose; it can be fun to do; it is an efficient use of training time; you can create a circuit indoors or outdoors; you can do it with little or no special equipment.

**14 (a) (i)** flexibility **(ii)** health-related **(b)** *Any one of these or similar examples:* flexible shoulders help a swimmer do the front crawl better; flexible hip, knee and ankle joints help a sprinter increase his or her stride; a flexible spine helps a gymnast do a smooth somersault. **(c)** In active stretching you stretch your own muscles.In passive stretching someone else stretches them for you.

**15 (a)** Warms the muscles and makes them more flexible, so there is less risk of muscle damage; warms and loosens the joints, which helps protects them from damage; increases heart rate and blood flow, so your muscles are getting plenty of oxygen; gets you mentally prepared for action. **(b)** Loosens tight muscles so they won't feel stiff later *or* prevents soreness of muscles.

**16 (a)** injury (including chronic injury), fatigue **(b)** Because the athlete is not competing, a chronic knee injury has more chance of recovery. The athlete can make time for physiotherapy and rehabilitation exercises. **(c)** An athlete might need to go abroad to train for any of these reasons: for better facilities (for example for some winter sports); to work with a particular coach; to prepare for a major event in that country (for example the Summer Olympics). Training abroad often means adapting to a different climate. It may be expensive, so the athlete may need to look for a sponsor or a grant. He or she has to train in a new situation, away from friends and family, which could be difficult.

**17** The lungs: vital capacity increases; more capillaries form around the alveoli. The result is that more oxygen is available for the muscles. The leg muscles: more capillaries form inside them, so more blood reaches the muscle fibres, carrying oxygen; they get better at using fat for energy; they can work harder for longer. The leg bones: they grow stronger; the protective cartilage at the ends grows thicker.

**18 (a)** protein **(b)** carbohydrate **(c)** It can't be digested by the body. **(d)** The body can't absorb calcium without it. So lack of vitamin D means soft bones.

**19 (a)** A diet that provides sufficient energy, with the right mix of nutrients and fibre. **(b)** carbohydrate **(c)** You use up a certain amount of energy every day. This energy comes from food. If you eat more food than you need for energy, the extra is stored as fat and you'll put on weight. But if you eat just enough to balance your energy requirements, you will keep your weight steady.

**20** *Here you could choose anorexia, obesity, or any condition caused by shortage of a vitamin or mineral. (See page 37.) A typical answer would be:* Eating more than you need on a regular basis can lead to obesity. This is a severe overweight condition. The extra weight puts a strain on the heart, muscles, bones and ligaments. It can lead to back injuries, heart attacks and other problems.

## Part three: Learning and playing a sport

**1 (a) (i)** open skills **(ii)** *A typical example:* saving a goal in football **(iii)** The environment includes the weather, the pitch, the spectators, and most important of all, the other players. These are continually changing position and taking different actions. **(b)** In sport, a skill is an action or set of actions. Each attempt at a skill is a performance.

**2 (a)** A - decision-making; B - feedback. **(b)** Input is any information you receive about the situation, through your eyes, ears, skin, muscles and joints. (*There are many possible examples. Here is just one:* For example when batting in cricket you see the bowler bowling the ball at you. **(c)** In feedback. **(d)** To interpret the input and make a decision about what action to take, the brain scans the memory looking for similar situations from before.

**3 (a)** The information processing system has limited channel capacity. In other words, it has limited ability to process a lot of information. If you try to practice the complete new skill, the system may get overloaded. So you get confused. **(b)** Part practice **(c)** The front crawl (*or any similar example*). **(d)** Visual.

**4 (a)** Knowledge of performance: for example you are told about a fault in your swimming stroke. Knowledge of results: for example you are told how many seconds it took you to swim a length. (*You will probably have come up with other examples.*) **(b)** Feedback helps you discover what you are doing wrong, and how to put it right. (*Other possible answers:* it encourages you, it helps you set goals for improvement, it helps you identify where more training or practice is needed.)

**5 (a)** *Any two of:* personality, stress, arousal, motivation. **(b)** For sports, you need a balanced diet. If you overeat (and especially with fatty or sweet foods), you get fat. This means more weight to carry, so you move more slowly and get tired sooner. If you undereat, you will feel too weak and tired to perform well. Lack of a vitamin or mineral will also affect performance. For example an iron deficiency makes you feel tired. To provide the energy for sport, your diet should be mainly carbohydrate (at least 55%) from starchy foods. To improve their performance in endurance events, some athletes increase the amount of carbohydrate by carboloading. Athletes who do a lot of weight training often increase their protein intake, to help build and repair their muscles.

**6 (a)** It is a state of excitement and alertness. **(b)** *Any two of:* sweaty palms; faster heart beat; faster breathing; dry mouth; nervous shaky feeling in the legs; a sick feeling in stomach. **(c)** under-aroused. He or she is too laid back or bored to perform well. **(d)** Between B and C. **(e)** *Any two of:* a pep talk, a warm up, a bright noisy environment, a goal to achieve in the event, friendly or hostile reactions from the crowd.

**7 (a)** It is the driving force that makes you decide what to do, and how much effort to put into it. **(b)** The Wimbledon trophy is one example. (A nice fat cheque is another!) **(c) (i)** An unrealistic goal will put you off. **(ii)** An exciting goal will challenge you and keep you interested. **(d)** No, it is too vague.

**8 (a)** Rugby. You can see the players pushing, shoving and tackling each other. **(b)** By practising for hours every day, in a determined effort to succeed. **(c)** *The answer here depends on the sport you choose. Check it with your teacher.*

**9 (a)** *Any two of:* likes team sports; enjoys contact sports; enjoys sports with lots of action; likes excitement; gets bored in training; enjoys important events; gets bored with intricate skills; performs better at high levels of arousal; has a higher tolerance of pain than an introvert does. **(b)** *These would be a good choice:* fishing, hill walking.

**10 (a)** The lungs get clogged up with tar, so they can't take in so much oxygen. The carbon monoxide in cigarette smoke also combines with haemoglobin in blood, instead of oxygen, and this reduces the amount of oxygen the blood can carry. **(b)** If muscles don't get enough oxygen, they can't work so hard, and will tire easily. So the athlete will be unfit.

**11 (a)** anabolic steroids **(b)** weightlifting (or shot putt or wrestling, for example) **(c)** *Choose any two of these effects:* heart disease; high blood pressure; weak tendons and ligaments; infertility; cancer; the growth of facial and body hair in females; a deepened voice in females.

**12 (a)** cracked and itchy skin between the toes **(b)** Wear flip-flops or other footwear in changing rooms. Wash feet often and dry carefully between the toes. **(c)** Special ointment or pads from the chemist. **(d)** veruccas

**13 (a)** Check that his or her kit is in good order; wear the correct kit for the game (including any protective kit; do a warm up. (*Answers could also include:* tie back long hair; remove any jewellery that might get caught in equipment or clothing; cut long nails.) **(b)** *There are many examples to choose from, including:* no jewellery allowed during a match, except for a wedding ring taped to the finger (netball); if a scrum collapses, play must stop (rugby); shin pads must be worn (football); if you commit five fouls you will be sent off (basketball); a player bleeding from a cut must be sent off for treatment (netball, rugby, football). **(c) (i)** An injury that develops over time and lingers for a long time. **(ii)** Any one of these causes: overuse of muscles; overtraining; poor technique; poor equipment; unsuitable footwear. **(iii)** golfer's elbow.

**14** B.

**15 (a)** The casualty can't move the limb normally; the limb may look deformed; pain; swelling and tenderness around the injury; bruising develops. **(b)** You must not try to straighten the limb (or move the limb unnecessarily).

16 **(a)** A tear in a muscle or tendon, due to overstretching. **(b)** *Any two of:* Rest the leg as much as possible; use a bandage to compress and support the damaged area; apply an ice pack; elevate the leg.

17 **(a)** rest, ice, compression, elevation. **(b)** to reduce the blood flow to the injury, in order to reduce pain, swelling and bruising. **(c)** Tie a crepe bandage around the injured area. **(d)** *Any one of these:* a minor strain; a minor sprain; bruising from a collision or fall. **(e)** In these injuries, blood vessels get damaged. When the blood leaks into the tissue around the injury, it causes swelling and bruising.

18 **(a)** danger; response; airway; breathing; circulation. **(b)** When you shake the person gently by the shoulders and shout 'Can you hear me?' there is no response of any kind. **(c)** To make sure the person can't choke on the tongue or any other obstacle. **(d)** No. Your first concern should be for your own safety. So first check for dangers like falling debris or fire.

19 E, C, A, F, D, B.

20 **(a)** concussion **(b)** *Any two of:* unconsciousness; memory loss; confusion; a dazed or staring appearance; dizziness; a sick feeling; drowsiness.

## Part four: Sport in society

1 Leisure is your free time when you can do as you please. There are several reasons for the growth in leisure in our society. First, machines have taken over many jobs in the workplace, which means more people are unemployed, or in part-time work, or forced into early retirement. Second, machines have taken over many household chores, leaving more free time in the home. And third, thanks to a better standard of living and better health care, people are living longer. So there are more active elderly people around with free time to enjoy.

2 *Here are three benefits. You may come up with others.* Membership of the club will encourage the school leaver to keep fit. He or she will have access to a range of facilities in one building, usually including a weights room and swimming pool. The club will also provide the opportunity to meet people and make new friends.

3 Elderly people are usually slower, stiffer, and less strong than young people. So they tend to avoid activities like rugby, football, gymnastics and athletics, for which young people are more fit. But crown green bowling and golf are popular with the elderly, since they depend more on skill than strength or speed. Walking and swimming are also popular with elderly people because they can do these at their own speed.

4 *For each group, any two from the list would be acceptable. But you may have come up with other good ideas.*
**(a)** A toddlers' pool; a play area for toddlers; a mother-and-toddlers club so that the mothers can socialize; staff to supervise the toddlers, so the mothers are free to go for a swim, for example.
**(b)** Disabled parking; easy access; special changing facilities; special equipment to help the disabled enjoy activities - for example to help them enter and leave a swimming pool; tutors to help disabled people learn new activities. **(c)** A good cafe where they can socialize; competitive events to keep them interested; new and challenging activities; tuition in

different activities such as canoeing or scuba diving; social events such as parties and discos.

5 **(a)** It has five parts: the United Kingdom Sports Council, and four separate Sports Councils for England, Scotland, Wales and Northern Ireland. The Sports Council for England had 10 regional offices spread throughout the country. **(b)** Its aims are: to increase participation in sport and physical recreation; to increase the number and quality of facilities; to develop excellence in sport.
**(c)** *Any two of these activities:* it awards grants to teachers to take coaching courses; it awards grants from the Lottery Sports Fund to projects that link schools with local clubs; it encourages local companies to sponsor sport in schools.

6 **(a) (i)** The Central Council for Physical Recreation **(ii)** *Any two of these:* It provides legal help for members; it provides financial advice for them; it tackles issues of general concern to its members, such as doping in sport; it promotes British sport abroad. **(b)** *You should have got two of these:* The Lawn Tennis Association; The Football Association; The Amateur Swimming Association; The Amateur Athletics Association; The English Basketball Association. **(c)** *Any three of these:* to draw up the rules of the sport and prevent their abuse; to organize local and national competitions; to select teams for international competitions; to settle disputes within the sport; to manage and coach sports officials such as referees; to help develop facilities; to maintain links with similar organizations abroad.

7 **(a)** The International Olympic Committee. *Any one of these functions:* To select the cities where the Olympic Games will be held; to decide which sports will be included; to help plan the games; to lead the fight against doping in sport. **(b)** The Sports Aid Foundation. To provide grants for top athletes and promising young athletes (including disabled athletes).

8 **(a)** To improve the quality of coaching in sport, at all levels. **(b)** Advantages of a single big centre: experts from different areas (such as sports science, sports psychology, nutrition) would all be under one roof, so could exchange ideas easily; athletes from all sports would have equal access to these experts; athletes from different sports would meet and learn from each other; it would cost less to build one large centre than several smaller ones. The money saved could be used to make the facilities even better. Disadvantages: a single big centre might feel impersonal; it would be harder to manage than several smaller centres; all the expertise would be centred in just one part of the country, rather than spread around.

9 **(a) (i)** Of every £1 spent on a Lottery ticket, 5.6 p goes to the Lottery Sports Fund. This is managed by the Sports Council. Applications for grants for sports-related projects are submitted to the Sports Council by governing bodies, schools, sports clubs and so on. A panel studies the applications and decides which projects qualify for grants. Then the money is given out. **(ii)** For the right to broadcast sports events, in order to attract viewers. **(b)** *Any two of:* To promote the sport; to develop and improve sports facilities; to stage sports events; to run training courses; to pay for coaches, umpires and other officials; to fund teams for international events.

10 **(a)** To look after the club's finances. **(b)** *Any three of:* by charging a membership fee; by charging

match fees (for example charging to book a squash court); by running events such as barbeques and raffles; by finding a company to sponsor it; by selling sweatshirts and other merchandise.

11 **(a)** PE is carried out in lesson time, as part of the school timetable. Sport is extra-curricular: it is played during lunch break, after school or at weekends. **(b)** The school gets access to the club's facilities, and perhaps to its coaches. Students can take part in activities for which the school has no facilities of its own. The students also become familiar with the club and how it works, and may decide to join it when they leave school. This in turn will benefit the club. A club may also have access to the school's facilities - for example sports halls and playing fields.

12 **(a)** In the UK, the government does not directly support promising young athletes. Some may win a sports grant to a university, or to a centre of excellence. Some are taken on by professional clubs as apprentice players. But most have to find their own coaches and fund their own training. In China the situation is quite different. Promising young athletes are sent to sports schools (often as young as six), and receive special coaching. If they develop into excellent athletes, the state continues to support them while they train and compete. **(b)** The athlete may get free tuition and perhaps free accommodation. He or she will probably receive top-class sports coaching in excellent facilities, along with other promising athletes. This will help to develop the athlete's potential.

13 **(a)** Professionals play their sport full time and get paid for it. They earn their living from it. Amateurs do not get paid for playing their sport and usually need a job to support themselves. (But top amateurs are rewarded indirectly!) **(b)** It is an event in which anyone can compete, whether amateur or professional. **(c)** *Any one of these advantages:* It gives all the athletes in the sport the chance to compete against each other; amateurs may improve as a result of competing against professionals; amateurs may get the chance to become professional; prize money allows an athlete to work at a sport full time, without having to take on another job to earn a living; there is no longer any need for these sports to 'bend the rules' by rewarding amateurs with 'gifts' as payment. *Any one of these disadvantages:* money could become the main motivation for the athletes; in the struggle for prize money, the idea of fair play could go out the window; when money is the main motivation for athletes, they may ignore the sport's governing body; a small group of top athletes in the sport will get rich while the rest may struggle.

14 **(a)** *Any two of these or similar examples:* a sum of money; a sports scholarship; free kit; free food; free travel. **(b)** XCO receives publicity in return. The company's logo appears on the athlete's clothing. If the event is shown on TV the logo is seen widely. If the athlete wins it reflects well on the company. **(c)** *Any two of these:* Smoking kills. Smoking makes people unfit for sport. By sponsoring sports events, cigarette companies gain a lot of 'healthy' publicity. Any connection between cigarettes and sport may encourage young people to smoke.

15 It depends on the person! Some people enjoy watching a sports event in the comfort of their living room. TV can also provide features you don't get at the live event – for example interviews with athletes, and discussion of the tactics and strategy by experts. The TV cameras can get much closer to the action than spectators at the live event can. All these are advantages. But many fans still prefer the atmosphere, noise, excitement and emotion of a live event, and enjoy cheering, shouting and singing with the other spectators.

16 TV needs to show sports events (such as golf and tennis championships) in order to attract viewers. So it pays large sums to broadcast these events, and gives them a lot of publicity. The events then find it easy to attract sponsors, who will benefit from this publicity. The result is that the events can afford to offer large cash prizes to attract the best players. Because of TV coverage, the winning players become 'stars', and companies will pay them further large sums to appear in their ads and endorse their products.

17 Better media coverage means more people will start to take an interest in women's sports, and more women will start playing them. In addition, if women's sports are given more coverage on TV, they will find it easier to get sponsorship money. They can use this money to promote and develop the sport further.

18 **(a)** Spectators provide players with emotional support by cheering them on. They provide financial support by buying tickets to events, and club merchandise. Players in turn provide spectators with excitement and enjoyment. **(b)** In sports like rugby and football, which suit a high level of arousal, cheers and encouraging shouts from spectators can help an athlete's performance. However, an athlete can be put off by jeering and racist chants. In sports like gymnastics, which suit a low level of arousal, noisy spectators could ruin the athlete's concentration and spoil the performance. **(c)** They are no longer allowed to have perimeter fences, or spectators standing on terraces. Stadiums must be all-seater.

19 **(a)** A city gains world-wide publicity when it hosts the Summer Olympics. If they go well, it gains a great deal of prestige, which will pay off later in areas like trade and tourism. During the games the city gets an enormous number of visitors, and local businesses like hotels and restaurants can make a lot of money. In addition the city can make a profit on the games themselves, through ticket sales, sponsorship, the sale of TV broadcast rights and so on. Road, rail and other services are usually improved for the games, and new sports facilities built. All this will benefit the city long after the games are over. **(b)** *Any three of these disadvantages:* Security is a big problem, because the event may attract terrorists and other groups who want to take advantage of the publicity to air their grievances. A big international event is difficult to organize. It is expensive to put on, so there is a risk that the host will lose money. If the event is badly organized (for example if the transport services can't cope with all the visitors) there will be many problems. If the event is a failure the host will get plenty of bad publicity.

20 *You should have chosen any two of these games:* Montreal in 1976 (financial and political problems); Moscow in 1980 (political problems); Los Angeles in 1984 (political problems); Seoul in 1988 (political problems). *For details of the problems check on page 78.*

# Index

Bold entries show where a term is defined or explained.